The Silk Purse

The Silk Purse

A MEMOIR

Blanca...
gracias por tu apoyo.

Raquel Ortiz
11/12/05
Chicago

Raquel Ortiz

To order additional copies of this book, contact:
Xlibris Corporation
1-888-795-4274
www.Xlibris.com
Orders@Xlibris.com
20353

Contents

From the beginning of life we're taught to let go and it's always a struggle,
for as we grow, we're taught to hang on.
In writing this memoir I have done both.

Raquel Ortiz

Introduction

Two weeks after my live-in boyfriend and I decided he'd help get me pregnant, I became very ill, with a temperature of 104 degrees and what appeared to be flu symptoms. After fainting from dehydration I was rushed to Mt. Auburn Hospital where I awoke two weeks before my fortieth birthday, in April of 1985, to find my stomach swollen, not with child, but with a stapled scar that began at my belly button and ended just above my pubic hairline. A complete hysterectomy had been performed on me. They'd taken everything out, ovaries, tubes and uterus. Six weeks earlier I'd had a complete physical examination, including my annual internal, where my doctor declared I was fit and fine. Now, my biological clock had ticked and a part of me was gone forever.

A few weeks into my recuperation, my dearest friends gave me a surprise birthday party, my first. I blew out forty candles, thankful to be alive and loved, thankful to be surrounded by dear friends, yet feeling terribly empty and hollow inside. That's when the inexplicable ache in my heart, an ache that lasted fifteen years, began.

Not too long after that, Dasel decided to move up his plan to relocate to Los Angeles, so he could begin to work on feature films as a director of photography. We'd agreed he'd get me pregnant and then move out west, but now there was no need to wait and he was excited about a "potentially good development deal." Everybody who moves to LA from the East Coast does so for two reasons: They are sick of the blustery New England winters or they have a great development deal in the works. In Dasel's case, it was both. Knowing I'd had a terrible experience in Los Angeles in my childhood, he never asked me to go with him, though I later found out he really wanted me to. I sometimes look back upon that fact regretfully, for we had a good trusting relationship that might have blossomed into something even more wonderful and long-lasting.

Now my clock had "tocked"! I was without child, without my insides and without a partner. At the time I thought I'd been through the worse; little did I know that the Universe had quite a hellish year planned out for me!

Three months after my radical surgery, Mother's five-year battle with cancer accelerated, traveling north, depositing three more tumors in her brain. We spent our last Thanksgiving together that year in my new Cambridge condominium, which we'd found and fallen in love with together the previous summer. I distinctly remember that precious moment when we both opened the door to the second-floor apartment of a New England-style triple-decker building and simultaneously said, "*Este es*! This is it!" "But you haven't even gotten past the entrance," replied the realtor. "We know," we chimed, "but it feels right." And right it was. We unpacked the beautiful wooden guitar-shaped chimes Mother had bought for just this purpose on our weekend visit to Martha's Vineyard. We blessed them and placed them at the foot of the hallway, then walked in, scoped the place and joyfully made plans about what would go where for the next hour. That autumn I moved into my condo and placed the chimes on the entrance door.

After receiving the news about Mother's latest cancer, I surprised *Mami* by arriving at her Alhambra, California, doorstep on Mother's Day, wrapped in a bright red and gold ribbon. Though she clapped wanly like a just-awoken sleepy child, because she was so weak from chemotherapy, her eyes showed total glee. I was not prepared for the sallow color of her skin replacing a rich olive Caribbean complexion nor for the almost totally white, shortly cropped gray fuzz on her head, where once there was an abundance of thick, rich dark brown curly waves of hair. My robust, buxom, zaftig mother was now thin, pale and worn. We hugged and kissed and made the best of her surprise as I fought back my tears.

Four days later, on the morning of her sixty-second birthday, we rushed her to the City of Hope Hospital. Little did we suspect this would be her last birthday, much less that I would take Mother's hand in mine, hold it against my cheek while once more fighting back another flood of tears and proclaim the news we all dreaded. Everything around us stood still as if suspended. *Mami* grabbed my blouse with her left hand; we looked into each other's eyes searching and wondering, I about how to approach the subject, she needing to hear the declaration and yet dreading it. My mind raced. How do you tell someone you love they are about to die? What words do you use? What tone is best? Is there a "best" tone for this? How do you hold back the tears you can't hold back? You must, I told myself sternly, you must! Are you brave or do you crumble upon hearing the words your mouth utters echo in your ears? Where does the strength come from to state the truth she insisted you be the one to tell her, the truth you both know she doesn't really want to hear? Where do you find the courage to tell the woman who gave you life, that death is no longer a possibility, it is now a fact! After what seemed like an eternity,

I whispered, "*Mami,* you have three new tumors in your brain at the nape of your neck. There is nothing else the doctors can do except minimize the pain and keep you comfortable." The words reverberated in my ears as if someone else were saying them. *Mami* stared back at me eyes glistening, shocked, yet knowing.

My sister, Venus, disappeared days ago. She struggled with the pain in her usual way, hiding somewhere unknown to any of us, crying and licking her wounds by herself. How I longed to find her and hold her close so we could cry together, but she would have none of that. Once a week, Venus worked up the courage to face *Mami* and give me a break so I could go home, do laundry, and rest a little before returning to Mother's bedside. I didn't resent her inability to deal with it; the fact is, I understood. Her pain was my pain. We simply handled it differently. When I returned the next day, Venus would disappear again, squirreling off to some lonely corner to wallow in the misery of her impending loss. Perhaps it was a greater loss for her. Venus and her first child, Elizabeth, lived with *Mami* and *Papi* since she was four years old. The three of them raised her together. Monique, her second child, was born in that house as well. Venus had to bear this burden three times over.

And my dear *Papito,* that strong, six-foot tall, handsome, Cuban male with the bellowing voice, upon hearing the news, walked away whimpering, leaving me with the task of declaring this truth to Mother. For the rest of her stay in the hospital he'd visit her daily, but his visits were brief. He'd take *Mami*'s hand in both of his, lovingly look into her eyes like he did when they first met. After a few minutes he'd begin whimpering like a child—*Hay mi nena linda, mi bella Dina*—then kiss her on the forehead and mouth and leave sobbing. On the days I went home to freshen up, I'd find him seated in his favorite recliner, looking sad and helpless.

It was strange and haunting to see my strong *Papito*, my rock, now looking lost and vulnerable, like a little boy. *Mami* had prepared me, making it clear that *Papito* and Venus would behave just as they did, unable to be in death's presence for too long. *Mami* always knew this scene would play itself out this way. I knew it too!

So, why, if I was strong enough to be there for her, was I not prepared? Why did I cry? Why did the world stand still? Why was my resentment at having to bear this burden alone so strong? Once again, it was just the two of us, *Mami* and me, first at my birth and now, at her death, the cycle of life repeated. I know, "*Mijita, lo se*," she said as she laid her head on the pillow, closed her eyes and let the tears flow.

Like the good stubborn Taurus she was, *Mami* held on for fifty-five days. Fifty-five days of being fed intravenously till there were no more veins left to puncture. Fifty-five days of being pumped with morphine, a drug that dulled her mind but never totally subdued her pain. Fifty-five days of seeing sadness and sometimes even disgust in the eyes of the man she loved with her whole being, when he looked upon the ravaged body he'd kissed in adoration for thirty-seven years. Now, he couldn't bear to see her pain just as he couldn't bear to look upon the scar of her first mastectomy. Fifty-five nights of sleeping on an inflatable mattress on the floor by her bedside. Each day another drop of dignity lost, for now it was her daughter who changed her underwear and washed *la flor,* that private woman's flower no mother ever expects her child to look upon, much less wipe clean.

Every day I bathed and changed Mother's garments. I washed every part of her, her face, neck, arms, her right breast and the scar that replaced her left one, her stomach, legs and *la flor.* She was now the baby, and I the mother and caretaker. After her cloth bath, I'd comb her hair and lovingly smoothed blush on her cheeks and painted her lips. Twice daily I cleaned and rubbed aloe lotion on her bedsores. I sang to her "The Autumn Leaves" or *Alfonsina y El Mar,* two of her favorite songs. On Sundays, I read her the *New York Times* book review or told her stories. We had a pact that I would be there when she died. I was terrified to go to the bathroom or eat lunch away from her, fearing she would die alone while I was gone. How silly of me not to realize that she would honor our pact and wait till I was there. They do, you know. If dying people want you present at that pivotal moment they wait until you're there, and if they don't, they wait till you leave before they pass on.

Mother's stubbornness allowed her to hold on, waiting for her eleventh grandchild to be baptized. On the fifty-fourth day Monique was brought to the hospital dressed in her long, white-laced baptismal gown, so that Nana could verify that she had been blessed by God and pardoned of the cardinal sin with which Catholics are born. Monique gave her Nana a little bottle of holy water as proof that she had received the precious sacrament that absolved her of original sin.

On July 6, I awoke startled. A sound was missing, what was it? Mother's strained phlegm-filled wheezing had ceased. I jumped up and put my ear to her chest, it moved only slightly.

For almost two months now, I had fallen asleep to that sound, fervently praying for God to take her out of her misery one moment, then guiltily begging forgiveness because I'd sought death, the next. Every night, while *Mami* wheezed, I lulled myself to sleep to the sounds of the machines that kept her alive. As long as that wheezing sound continued, *Mami* was alive. But, this morning I couldn't hear it. It was quiet, much too quiet.

I leaped up from the air mattress and uncovered her legs. They were like marble, hard, ice cold, speckled with thick blue lines, as if the blood were seeping out of her veins. I looked up at her face, her lips moved, but no sound came out. Her eyes, wide open, shone like glass and looked straight at me. They told me everything. Her beautiful limp hands reached for my blouse, pulling me closer, spending her last bit of strength. I can't take the pain anymore. "*Me voy!*" she said. "Hold on" I said, "*Papito*'s on his way." "I can't, it's time! Kiss *Papito* for me. Take care of Venus and the girls. *Te quiero, Mi hija, Adiós!*"

She closed her eyes and went limp in my arms. I stood frozen tears gushing down my face. "She's gone" There is no greater sense of loss than the moment your mother goes. Neither the loss of my virginity, nor the loss of my ability to give birth, left so empty a feeling within me. My *Mami*, was gone, *para siempre!*

Though I'd had the five years during which this voracious cancer fed itself on her body to prepare for this moment, I wasn't ready even though I had slept by her bedside for the past two months; when it happened, I was stunned. And, I was relieved. My prayers were answered. She was out of pain. Strangely, I felt no guilt this time.

About a month after *Mami* passed on, my biological father, Angel, also died. I was told he went peacefully in the middle of the night. I felt rage well up in me at his good fortune, while Mother suffered so terribly and for so long. Why should he who caused us so much pain make his transition quietly and peacefully?

But, it was not over yet—the saga of the losses of my fortieth year continued. Two months later, my ex-husband, Roy, who remained a dear friend even though we were divorced, died as he wished, in his sleep. I'm glad he got his wish. And, the final blow came with the death of a dear friend and leader in the Boston Latino community who died of AIDS. It had been a hellish year, the kind that makes you stop and think and ask yourself, what have I left undone? My writing!

The idea that I should write emerged while Mother and I tied up the loose ends of her life during her last days at the

City of Hope Hospital. In between finalizing her will, calling her dearest friends and arranging for her resting-place, we'd have long talks about my work as a producer and host of *La Plaza* at WGBH, the stories I wanted to work on, and my dreams and goals for the future. Yet, fourteen years were to pass before I put pen to paper. Once I returned home after *Mami*'s death, I threw myself into my work again, using it as salve for the pain of her loss. It wasn't too long before I once again faced two difficult life situations. Now, it was my dear *Papito*, who was diagnosed with Alzheimer's disease. He asked that I become conservator of his estate. And, if managing that difficult and daunting task wasn't enough, I myself was struggling with the insidious depression that was steadfastly taking over my emotional state.

The fall of 1993 offered a bright moment in this difficult decade. My friend Margot invited me to join her on a trip to Santa Fe, New Mexico, a place I instantly fell in love with. While visiting the Pueblo Indian site, I turned to Margot saying, "This is where I want to write my book." As I finished uttering those words, a gold bracelet with the small onyx *asabache* stone my mother left me in her will, fell into the sacred river. I stared at it glistening in the clear water and felt an inner calm. Though I'd lost a precious memento, I knew deep within me it was *Mami* saying, *Si, Mijita*, yes my darling!

Shortly after that miraculous experience, I was awarded a MacDowell Artist Colony residency where I finally began putting words on paper. After that exquisite but brief six-week interlude, I returned to the real world, and again, my writing was placed at the end of the priority list. Finally, in May of 1999, two incidents sealed my fate. On my fifty-fourth birthday, while languishing on a hammock underneath a flowing palm tree at the mountaintop home of friends in Caimito, Puerto Rico, musing about my future, I had an epiphany. I began reviewing milestones in my life; Mother died in 1986, Father died in 1994. *Two years have passed since my time at MacDowell. Coño, today I'm fifty-four and the book is still unwritten.* I leapt out of the hammock and yelled out to the plantain trees: "*Ortiz, it's time to stop saying—I'munna do this and I'munna do that.* Write the book, girlfriend. Take a leap of faith, give yourself a sabbatical, go to New Mexico, and do it already."

The second epiphany came about a week later back home in Cambridge. During one of my organizing purging sessions, I came upon the heart shaped fifties-retro carton box covered in peonies where I kept mementos and old birthday cards. Inside was the only letter Mother wrote me. In the faint, penciled handwriting of a dying woman, her English not at its best, she wrote:

> *Dearest daughter of my heart and of my soul that you always were. One has many children, all you love, each for different reasons. Your sister was that which comes from immense passion, admiration, love and beauty that existed between her Dad and me till today. He was my Adonis, and I guess, I was his Venus. That's why she got her name, because of that consuming love we had and even now have for each other.*
>
> *But you were my dream of a copy of myself, maybe because I was young and foolish and life had hurt me, and I didn't know how to give the correct way, so I made very bad mistakes. You, for different reasons than Venus, would have your Knight in shining armor to win and protect you. Little did I know that that Knight would be yourself. And how well, daughter, you fought your battles with honor and decisions. You are all I dreamed of being and that's why you are the daughter of my innermost heart and soul.*
>
> *Well, my beloved Rae. I've never written you a letter but this one I hope will help you understand me in relationship to you. You have given me beautiful gifts for my soul to live on*

*apart from the material ones. And these I cherish the most. I
hate to leave you, your brothers and Venus and Papi and the
girls.*

Love, Mom.

P.S. Remember to write your stories!

*Enedina Castaño de Santiago
Passed away July 6, 1986*

The words, "Remember to write your stories," resonated
in my head as I recalled a conversation we'd had during her
last days in the hospital. I could hear her gentle loving voice
clearly.

"You should write your stories, darling, stories about our
family, about being Puerto Rican and Cuban, and then you
should produce them. Don't forget, it's important. That's
your legacy, *querida!*"

"But *Mami*, I'm a producer not a writer."

"Well dear, you're the one who told me producers have
to write it before they can produce it."

"Yes," I replied, "but it's not that kind of writing, this is
drama."

"So," she said, "you can learn can't you?"

That conversation became like a seed that she had
planted and it had been germinating all this time. Losing
the bracelet in New Mexico was her way of reminding me to
get it done.

Suddenly, all doubts melted away with the postscript in
Mother's letter. The next day I gave notice at work. Two
months later, my Cambridge apartment was sublet, I withdrew
my savings, packed my luggage and my long-haired black
cat Midnight and drove the 2,040 miles to Santa Fe, New
Mexico. Six days later, I arrived at the apartment I'd leased
on Old Pecos Road, unpacked, set up my computer and
began to write.

Though it was not always easy and often excruciatingly painful, the catharsis of writing has been an enriching and rewarding experience. I came to understand both sides of my relationship with Mother. And, I found that when I wrote, I'd get lost in my work. I'd start early in the morning, and before I knew it, the day had gone by and the sun was beginning its decline. I could not now conceive of dying without having completed this memoir, and in doing so, I've found my new work, my new path.

1

A NEW PAPITO

My first jolt in my life was the kick to my mother's blossoming belly from my biological father's army boot during one of his drunken binges while on military leave. I call him my "biological father," because all he did was plant his sperm in mother's belly and then gave us both a good swift kick. Mother was rushed to Lincoln Hospital, and I arrived five months early one May morning in 1945, weighing five-and-a-half pounds, looking skinny, scrawny and ugly. A "preemie". I'm told I looked that way for a long time! Years later when I was ten, family members still stared at me, amazed that I had survived that turbulent welcome into the world. So am I!

It was 1945 the allied forces were on their final path into Germany and Japan would be jolted into surrender by the explosion of the atomic bomb.

Back home *Mami* was jolted into action as well. "That was it. "S*e acabo!*" She later passed on her first important lesson regarding men to me. "If a man hits you once he'll hit you twice", don't make my mistake, get out after the first whack." While I was still in the incubator she packed our stuff, and along with my brothers, Junior and Victor, went to live with her parents in their basement apartment in El Barrio, and my "biological father" was swiftly catapulted out of my life.

Of course, Angel Sr., begged her to return, but mother said, *"Jamas,* never! If you hit me again I'll have to kill you, and I don't intend to spend my life in jail, so forget it." Once she made up her mind it was unchangeable. Such was the case when at age sixteen she ran off with him, tired of living under the strict watchful eyes of her parents and great aunt, Titi María. *Mami* was beautiful, with a lush body and deep dark eyes. She was also very smart, spoke both Spanish and English excellently and played the violin. She often told the story of her teacher who came to their house to speak with her parents and encourage them to allow *Mami,* whom she considered to be musically gifted, to pursue a musical career. But, in those days, young Catholic Puerto Rican girls, gifted or not, weren't allowed to pursue musical careers. They got married and had children, and that's just what *Mami* did. At sixteen, four months before graduating high school, she eloped with Angel Ortiz, Sr. Three years later she had three children, was separated from her husband and living with her parents in a tiny basement apartment.

Month after month Angel came around sheepishly trying to cajole *Mami* to return. They'd have loud screaming fights about his wanting the boys, and a few times he'd raise his hands toward *Mami,* but he'd never hit her in front of *Abuelo,* who swore he'd kill him. Eventually he relented, accepting his loss. *Mami* softened as well, and they agreed that for the time being he should keep my brothers, Victor and Angel Jr., a decision that would haunt her the rest of her life. I would stay with *Mami* and *Los Abuelos,* with whom we lived the first three years of my life. Not long after they made that decision, Angel Sr., and my brothers disappeared. For years after that *Mami* would save a dollar each day to pay a private detective to help find them. I hadn't even reached my first birthday and already my life was filled with trauma, pain and loss.

Fortunately, *Los Abuelos* were very loving. *Abuelo*'s name was Don Domingo Santiago Gouglas. He was the super of the building on 110th Street, which is why we lived in the basement. *Abuela*'s name was Doña Adelaida Santiago-Rivera. Such aristocratic names for people who lived in the bowels of a building between the boiler room and the garbage cans, I thought. The only window we had in the living room looked up at the world, not out. I saw people from the knees down, calves, ankles and shoes walking by. Maybe that's why I developed my love of shoes. Through this tiny window, it was hard to tell if the sun was shining. The sky always looked gray. When it rained, the drops crashed on the pavement splitting into a thousand miniature diamond drops.

Abuelo was tall, skinny and had supple, delicious cinnamon—colored skin. He was bald and always wore his hat. Summer, winter, fall or spring, whether indoor or outside, *Abuelo* never took his hat off until his last act of the day before turning out the lamp and saying "Bendición, mis nenas," (Bless you my girls).

Abuela's skin was creamy colored, and her face was wonderfully wrinkled. The crevices were deep, yet soft to the touch. She had green eyes and thick long salt-and-pepper gray hair, that she kept wrapped in a *redencilla*. She always wore a hairnet, a thick one at home and at work, and a thin delicate one for going to Church. *Abuela* was short, exactly five feet, and always had to look up at *Abuelo* when speaking to him. With her left hand on her hip, and her right pointing a finger at him, she'd say, Don Domingo, this or Don Domingo that. I think she pointed her finger as a way of showing him who was really the boss. They always addressed each other in the formal way, with the Don and Doña. "Por favor, Don Domingo, come here please." He'd walk toward

her responding, *"Si Señora", or "Si Doña Adela,"* with a smile
that crinkled the lines around his small brown eyes. It was as
if they were always sharing a secret and having fun with each
other.

Abuela arose at 4:00AM every morning, went directly
into the kitchen, and began her daily ritual of brewing the
morning coffee. She'd boil the water, put three huge
spoonfuls of coffee grains into the cotton strainer, pour in
hot water and squeeze the dark black liquid into a *pocillo*—
a small demitasse cup. Then she'd take the cup along with
a glass of water to *Abuelo* in bed. *Abuelo* would rinse his
mouth with a big gulp of water, which he'd gurgle noisily
and spit out into the *escupidera*. Then he'd slowly sip his
strong black *"Café Bustelo"* while watching *Abuela* put on
her starched white uniform. He'd finish his *cafecito,* wash
up and get dressed, while grandma prepared our breakfast
and lunch. *Abuelo* walked grandma to the station every
morning. Rain, snow or shine, she boarded the train for
Brooklyn and walked five blocks to her job at the public
school where she continued preparing food, this time it
was lunch for the students.

I began my days secretly and happily observing this
morning ritual. *Abuelo* and *Abuela* thought I was asleep, but
the rich smell of grandma's coffee always woke me up. I'd
pull the covers over my head and listen as they gently
muttered to each other about what grandma would make
for dinner and what time *Abuelo* should meet her at the
station that evening. Next, it was *Mami's* turn to get ready
for work while I dozed off. She usually left when *Abuelo*
returned, and then it was my turn to get ready. Once I was
dressed, *Abuelo* and I would eat breakfast together then take
our morning walk in Central Park.

Abuela only went to four places; to work, to *La Marketa*,
to Church and to visit her *Santera*. Usually I accompanied

Abuela on her visits to see Doña Yoli, but I was never allowed in the room while *La Santera* was performing her miracles. I'd sit in the foyer, my nostrils taking in the wafts of incense that smelled just like what they burned in Church on Sundays before giving out the Holy Communion wafer, listening to the rumbling and mumbling of Doña *Yoli's* chants. She'd call to *"Ochún,"* the saint of the world's riches and rivers, and *"Yemalla,"* the Goddess of the Sea, or any of the other saints in her deep throaty male-sounding voice. In the background I'd hear the sound of African drums as Doña *Yoli's* incantations cleansed *Abuela's* worries away. Once done, they'd invite me to join them as they sipped their medicinal sherry together and I had a *Malta* (non-alcoholic malt beer). *Abuela* would always leave these sessions looking relaxed and smiling.

Our three-room railroad apartment in the basement was long and dark, with a small window in the living room that looked out onto the sidewalk and a big one in the kitchen. You entered in the living room and walked through all three rooms toward the kitchen. Our living room served two purposes. In the daytime we sat, talked and listened to the radio, and at night it was a bedroom for *Mami* and me. It held the day-bed sofa, grandpa's rocking chair, and a bureau with a small radio that rested on top of a lovely handmade doily. The lowest of the bureau's five drawers had my first bed until I outgrew it and began sharing the daybed with *Mami*. This was great fun, for we'd snuggle up close as *Mami* told me a story before I went to sleep. Above the breakfront that faced us there were three pictures that were their own personal shrine. In the center was Jesus Christ with a crown of thorns around his head, on the left was a picture of *Luis Muñoz Marín,* the first elected Governor of Puerto Rico, and on the right was the Arch-Angel watching over two kids crossing a bridge. These pictures hung in every home *Abuelo* and *Abuela* lived in. The Archangel now hangs in my bedroom and *Abuelo's* rocking chair graces my kitchen. When I was older they added a picture of President John F. Kennedy, Jr., to the collection.

From the living room, you walked through *Abuela* and *Abuelo*'s narrow bedroom. On the left was their bed and on the right was grandma's three-mirrored vanity, called a *tocador.* On it was the mother-of-pearl brush and comb set *Abuelo* gave *Abuelita* when they married. Often, my last task in the evening would be to gently brush her long silver hair with it.

The walls were painted white, but they always looked gray and dingy because there was so little light and so much dusty soot from the boiler that hummed throughout the night helping to lull us to sleep.

The last room in the house was the kitchen. We spent most of our time in there because it was big and warm and had a large window and door that opened into the back yard. Our dining table was placed in front of this window. Its top was made of porcelain, white with blue trim that rested on a heavy carved wooden base. The top had flaps that opened out on each side for expansion, and a little drawer where I kept pencils, crayons and paper to draw on while *Abuela* cooked. *Abuela* would hum romantic boleros of her Puerto Rican youth by *"EL Trio Los Panchos"* while making the house smell delicious, and I'd happily draw pictures of her and *Abuelo*. Over time I learned many of these songs and joined *Abuela* in her reverie.

Our bathtub was also in the kitchen, right next to the stove and sink. It was long and oval-shaped with animal paws for legs and was covered with a heavy porcelain top, where *Abuela* prepared food and drained the dishes during the day. At night, the cover was removed and the tub was filled with buckets of hot water that grandma boiled for our baths. I bathed first, then *Mami*, and then *Abuela*. For the next hour or so, it would be just us girls, *Abuela*, *Mami* and me. The radio would play *Abuela*'s favorite "bolero" love songs while she poured the warm water over my head and shoulders, then rubbed my back with a wash cloth while I made bubbles. Like a gentle waterfall she'd rinse off all the suds, then *Mami* would pull me out of the tub and rub me dry with a warm towel, tickling me into hysterics in the process. After that it was my turn to shower *Abuelita*. By the time *Mami* took her bath, I was often fast asleep. Grandpa refused to go through that trouble every night, so he usually bathed every other night, and just washed himself with a cloth after we were all in our beds. When he was through he'd put the cover back on the tub, check the locks on the doors, turn down the boiler and turn out the lights. He was always the last to go to sleep.

Underneath the kitchen cabinets on the opposite wall, was the wooden icebox with three doors, where we kept our milk, eggs, butter and chicken. The section for the ice had the biggest door, with two smaller doors underneath. The Iceman came twice a week, on Saturdays and Wednesdays to deliver a huge block of ice. He'd park his truck in front of our building, wiping out the little sunlight we'd get. Then he'd wrap a block of ice in dark brown burlap, pick it up with two big metal hooks and walk through our apartment to the kitchen, leaving a trail of icy drops which *Abuela* mopped up behind him, until he placed it in the icebox. Mr. Joe was muscular and sweaty, but friendly, and always gave me a lollipop before he left.

The ice section was so big that there wasn't much space left for the food items, so *Abuelo* built a second wooden box right outside our kitchen window. In the winter we could store a lot more items in that box because it was so cold outside. *Abuela* liked the luxury of opening the kitchen window and taking whatever she needed, because it saved her trips to the store in the cold winter days. I thought it was pretty smart and unique of grandpa to do that, though later I discovered everyone in the building had both a window box and a kitchen ice box. In the summer, we'd keep fewer staples in the house because there just wasn't enough space, but it was warm, so going to *La Marketa* was more pleasant.

Grandma kept the kitchen window covered with pretty white curtains, so that we'd get the light, but wouldn't have to see the junk people dumped in the back yard. No matter how hard *Abuelo* worked to keep it clean, people used the back yard as their personal dumping ground: stained torn mattresses, broken chairs, car parts, bottles, cans, chicken bones. They'd walk their dogs and leave the "poop" everywhere. Once a week grandpa spent an entire day cleaning it up, but by the end of the week it was again filled with garbage. Being El Super was endless, repetitive, tedious hard work.

Our "toilet bowl" room was on the far side of the basement after the boiler room, meaning you had to walk in the dark to find it. Even though this room was next to the boiler, it was always cold so when I sat on it I got goose bumps all over. I hated going to the toilet bowl room. I preferred to use my personal porcelain pee pot, which was kept under my bed. It was intended only for nighttime use, but I used it whenever I needed to go so I could avoid going to that frigid bathroom.

Shortly after we moved in with *Los Abuelos, Mami* found a job working with her cousin *Titi Argelia* at Saks Fifth Avenue, a fancy store downtown. *Titi Argelia* was a seamstress, and *Mami* modeled the clothes she and other ladies made. Sometimes I'd see pictures of *Mami* in fancy expensive clothes and imagined we lived on Park or Fifth Avenue in the places where she modeled them. *Mami* left early in the morning and I wouldn't see her until she arrived at night for dinner. Dinner was the one meal we tried to eat together. If she was late, grandma would save her a plate, and then I'd sit with *Mami* while she ate. We didn't have telephones then, so she couldn't call to let us know what time she'd arrive.

During the week I'd spend the whole day following *Abuelo* around the house. When we returned from his morning constitutional *caminada,* he would sit in his rocker, remove his shoes and socks, and listen to the news on the radio while rubbing his feet. I would sit on the sofa and rock listening to *Abuelo* comment on the news. Though I understood the words, I wasn't always clear what he was talking about, but we kept each other company. He had become my *Papi*, so I really didn't miss Angel, Sr., but I often wondered about my brothers. How were they, where were they?

On Saturdays, *Abuela* cleaned the apartment and made the grocery list. Then we'd go to *La Marketa* to buy the week's rations; milk, bread, yucca, *plátanos*, herbs, and chicken, when she could afford it. We'd also visit her *Santera* friend, *Doña Yoli*, (short for *Yoland) a* who sold candles and potions and *alcolado* for grandma's headaches. Alcolado was a pungent smelling mixture of alcohol, eucalyptus and other herbs that *La Santera* made for *Abuela's* headaches. She'd pour the liquid onto a long white cloth and wrap it around her forehead until the headache went away, which sometimes took three or four days. They're the kind of headaches that today we call "migraines".

After two years of living with *Los Abuelos*, mother found a new boyfriend. He was Cuban: Sr. Pedro Andrés Manuel Castaño de Vasquez. *Abuelo* was worried. He believed you should stick to your own kind and said Cubans were "uppity". *Abuela* was happy for *Mami*. Yet, when they decided to get married, she insisted I remain living with her and *Abuelo* for at least a year. *Abuela* said they needed time by themselves to enjoy *el romance* before bringing me to live with them, and I needed to get to know my new "*Papito*" slowly. But *Abuela* told me secretly that she really wanted to be sure he wasn't going to hit her or be *abusivo* like my real father. I was perfectly happy living with *Los Abuelos*, and liked *Abuela's* idea of slowly getting to know *Mami's* new man. At first I thought I'd miss *Mami*, but I didn't because she would stop by two or three times a week for dinner and we'd play or she'd read me a story. I'd also spend part of the weekend

with them as they usually came by on Sunday afternoons
and take me to Central Park, then we'd have dinner with
Los Abuelos.

   The year of waiting while *Mami* and *Papito* had their
honeymoon period swept by quickly, and soon it was time
for me to move in with them. *Abuela* and I observed closely
and found that *Mami* never had any bruises and she never
came home crying. I soon came to trust and fall in love with
my new *Papito.* I was excited about living with Mami and my
new Papito, but I was also ambivalent about this impending
change. I loved living with *Abuelo* and *Abuela* and doing all
our usual things together: the walks in Central Park, listening
to the news and *Las Novelas,* going to *La Marketa* and visiting
Doña Yoli. I was their pride and joy and they gave me lots of
loving attention. Why would I want to give that up? What I
really wanted was for all of us to live together. *Abuela* agreed
with me but said the new apartment was too small.
   For this first visit to my new home, *Abuela* dressed me up
in my only pretty pink Sunday dress with matching socks,
and my *zapaticos de charol,* black patent leather Mary-Jane
shoes. She took the tightly wrapped brown paper strips out
of my hair to reveal bouncing auburn ringlets, then added a
matching pink ribbon on top. I hated those ribbons in my
hair, they stuck out like wings, but on this day I didn't
complain because I was so excited about the trip to a place
I'd never been to before.

   Next came breakfast, a big one. One of *Abuela*'s rules
was that she insisted on our having a good breakfast. If you
ate a hearty meal at the beginning of the day, you'd have
plenty of *energía* to learn to work and play. That was her
motto. Breakfast consisted of oatmeal or *funche* (cornmeal),
a hard-boiled egg, *tostada criolla* and my favorite *café con leche.*

If you ask me, it was really make-believe coffee: a big cup of steaming frothy hot milk with two drops of café, but I loved it because it made me feel grown-up.

All dressed up, stuffed, fidgety and excited, *Abuela* sat me down to wait for *Mami* and my "New *Papito*". I sat on the sofa and began rocking back and forth, thinking: "How far is not too far?" What would it be like to live with my New *Papito*? Would I still have to sleep on the new living room sofa or would I have a room of my own? And, most important, would he be nice to *Mami*?

At last they arrived. I leaped out of the sofa into *Papito*'s arms. I liked him. Whenever he came to visit us, he always told me a story, in Spanish, and paid more attention to me than to *Mami*, though he was always sneaking loving glances at her when he thought I wasn't looking. I twirled around for *Mami* so she could see how pretty I looked in the dress she made me. She beamed with pleasure.

My new *Papito* was kind, gentle and very, very handsome. He had a fine thin nose, his dark eyes slanted upward, and he slicked his black hair back in a dramatic "v-shape style" like Rudolph Valentino, which *Mami* called his *entradas*. When he looked at you with his onyx eyes, it felt as if he saw deep into your soul. That must be how *Mami* felt when he gazed at her adoringly, which he did a lot.

In our home, after being greeted warmly with hugs and kisses, you were always offered *un cafecito*. So, anxious though I was to see my new home, *Papito* sat down and slowly sipped his miniature cup of coffee, while I fidgeted waiting to go on my new adventure. When he finally finished, the hugging and kissing began all over again, as if they weren't going to see each other for months, which added another twenty minutes to our departure. Finally we were on our way.

Up until that day, I had only ventured out to three places, all of them close by. There was the front stoop where *Abuela* could watch me play through the upward facing window; Central Park, with *Abuelo* on his daily morning walk, and to *La Marketa* on 116th Street every Saturday for *Abuela*'s weekly shopping spree where her *Santera* friend, Doña Yoli, lived. Oh, and church on Sundays, but that was just across the street.

My favorite place was *La Marketa*, where every Puerto Rican woman bought her special condiments and products from the Island. It was the only place in the city you could find them in those days. Women would travel to *La Marketa* from Brooklyn, Queens, The Bronx and even Staten Island every week so they could buy items like *plátanos, yautia* and *yucca* (root vegetables), as well as green limes and tomatoes; things they couldn't get nice and fresh in a corner grocery store or market. There were exotic herbs and spices, like *recau, cilantro, comino and ajies dulces,* sweet little rosebud-like peppers with lots of seeds, the ingredients that made *Abuela*'s kitchen smell so good. The odors from her cooking invaded my nostrils every day, instantly making me ravenous. My world was rich with *Abuelo*'s daily walks and story telling and *Abuela*'s loving *cariño* and delicious *comida criolla,* though it was about to change.

On my new adventure I walked in the center between *Mami* and my new *Papito.* As we strolled down the street, they looked at each other above me, and I looked ahead and from side to side. Some things I saw were the same as on my block: boys playing baseball, girls jumping rope and mothers sitting on the front steps chatting, with one eye on their knitting and the other on their kids. Other things were different, like some really tall buildings that made me turn my head all the way backward to see them.

We stopped at a corner. "Fifth Avenue" *Mami* said, as she pointed to the sign. I looked up at the sign, then across to the other side. I'd never seen an Avenue this big before.

It was wide, with lots of white lines. I counted five with many cars in each lane going fast and in both directions. There were regular sized cars, and long ones with lots of windows that I had never seen before. *Mami* called them buses, and said people who didn't have cars traveled on them to get to work. The light changed to green and we started to walk to the other side. I looked to my right and left, like I had been taught, but when I saw all those cars speeding toward us, I froze and right there in the middle of the lane I sat down and started screaming at the top of my lungs. Suddenly there were loud screeching sounds, among them *Mami*, who was yelling, *"Pedrito,* pick her up, *cójela"*. He picked me up and ran across the street, but it wasn't over yet!

While we waited for *Mami* to cross the avenue and join us, I suddenly heard a thunderous sound. I looked up at the sky to see if it was going to rain. Thunder and lighting scared me, but this sound didn't come from the sky, it came from underneath my feet. I looked down through a grate into a dark hole. The sidewalk began to tremble like an earthquake was about to break open and a thunderous roar pierced my ears. I covered them yelling "no, no, take me back to *Abuela.* "There's a *monstro* down there, please take me back to *Los Abuelos."*

Papito held me tight and carried me down those dark stairs. At least now the monster was quiet. He stopped and gave money to a man in a glass box. I wrapped my arms around his neck like a snake holding on tightly as he walked through the turnstile and into the monster hole. Then I heard the thunderous monster roar again and dug my face into *Papito*'s neck. I peeked through one eye and saw many long dingy dark gray boxes with windows swooshing by really fast. It looked like a huge monstrous version of my brother's train set but was much louder. It stopped with a sharp screech that made me wince. The doors separated. *Papito* and *Mami* stepped into the subway train and sat down. I hid my face in *Papito*'s neck again, whimpering like a lost puppy throughout the entire trip. *Mami* patted my head saying "Don't cry *Mijita, no llores,* "as I listened to the monster's roar from inside. After a long time, we got off and went through another turnstile. This time I asked *Papito* to go around twice. It was the only part of the train ride I liked.

As we climbed up the stairs into the light, I looked up and saw another sign. It said Ortiz and something else. That was my last name up there and *Mami*'s too. As we walked toward the building, I asked *Mami* "Is this where we're going to live?" "*Si Mija*", she said. "What are the other two words, next to our name?" "Funeral Parlor", she said. "It's where they visit dead people before they're buried. "Dead people, we're going to live with dead people." Now I really wanted to go back to home to *Abuela*. Before I could start another crying tantrum in public, *Papito* picked me up, opened the door and walked into a hallway.

Inside, there were many closed doors with golden numbers on them. *Mami* opened number three and *Papito* walked in. It was dark, with church music playing. In the room was a long shiny brown wooden box. There were tall candles on each side of the box and lots of flowers, orange gladiolas and white carnations in front. As we walked closer to the box, I could feel my heart thump like it had grown bigger. When we got really close, I saw a wrinkled lady with silver hair sleeping in the box. Her head lay on a creamy shiny satin pillow. She was very still, and wore a frilly blue dress and had a rosary wrapped around her hands, which were crossed over her heart. *Papito* spoke into my ear in his gentle story-telling voice, "*Ves, está durmiendo,* she's sleeping." This is her last stop on earth before going to heaven." He leaned over and caressed the lady's face. I put my hands under my armpits, looked at him sideways, my lips pursed tightly and shook my head emphatically.

Now I know why *Abuela* was always so afraid when I went outside to play. It was dangerous out there. We had only traveled six blocks on my first new adventure beyond 110th Street, which I thought was going to be fun, but instead had turned out to be pretty scary. I'd seen cars zooming past me and buses racing toward me, heard a dragon growling in a dark hole trembling under my feet, and learned we were going to live with dead people. I didn't care if I was going to have my own room anymore, and I was beginning to wish *Mami* hadn't married my *Papito*. I just kept repeating, "*Yo quiero a Abuela,* I want *Abuela.*"

But adults always have the last word and the following week we moved into the apartment above the Ortiz Funeral Parlor on 105th Street. This time the trip was less scary since *Papito* let me ride in the moving truck with him and *Mami,* and when we got there, we went up the stairs into the apartment instead of through the funeral parlor door. I immediately sat by the front bay window and watched *Papito* and *Abuelo* as they moved things into the apartment. I enjoyed looking out of this window because it jutted out a little so I could see clear to the corner on both sides. There were beautiful tall black wrought-iron street lamps on all four corners, a blue mailbox on our side of the street, *La Bodega de la Esquina* (the corner store) and *La Farmacia* for medicines. It was a busy street with lots of people coming and going, especially the women who visited the bridal dress shop with pastel colored "frufru" dresses in the window.

As I sat there, I felt happy and scared and sad all at the same time. I was happy to be together in our new home with *Mami* and my new *Papito,* yet scared about living above dead people. But mostly, I was sad because I already missed *Abuela* and *Abuelo,* even though they were here with us right now. They only lived five blocks and three avenues away, but I wouldn't see them every morning and we wouldn't share our daily rituals, which made me unhappy. Luckily, as it turned out, I was wrong about that because I spent every day with *Los Abuelos* while *Papito* and *Mami* went to work.

What I remember most about living above the funeral

parlor is that it was a sad place to be. Every week these long dark cars with dark gray windows that I couldn't see through arrived in front of our building. Men and women would come out of the cars dressed in black clothes. The women had white lace handkerchiefs touching their noses as they whimpered or sobbed. I never saw anybody laugh when they came out of these funeral cars.

Once the crying people were inside, *Papito* would come out and help the driver take out the long dark coffin and together they'd place it on a rack with wheels and bring it inside. I was not allowed on the first floor where the sad people sat and stared at the dead people for hours. Yet, in spite of this rule and my fear, I couldn't resist sneaking down and taking a peek as the sad people muttered to each other in whispers. "Doesn't she look good," one would ask, the other replying, "Oh yes, they did a fine job." Or "Oh look at the beautiful flowers so and so sent!" "That was her favorite color, she looks just like she did in real life," and then they'd start crying again. Some people would cry out loudly as if in pain, then throw themselves wailing onto the coffin, begging God to take them too. Why I wondered, why would they want to be in a box and why would they want to be dead when they could be alive?

Papito caught me a few times and scolded me, but I kept sneaking in to see these strange family visits. Since I loved staring out of the window, *Papito* built a lovely window seat for me where I spent the better part of my day. I would sit and play with my only doll, named *Doña Missy*, or my coloring books, but my favorite thing was to gaze out of the window and watch people come and go. Whenever a long shiny black hearse parked in front of our building, I'd stare at them as they got out, trying to decide if they were going to be quiet criers or wail passionately. I loved the ones who wailed because they were so dramatic.

When one of my mother's aunts, *Tia Juana-Inez*, lost her husband, *Tio Guillo,* he was brought to our funeral parlor. She was a wailer! I'd never seen anyone sob as loud or as

long as *Titi Juana-Inez* did. No matter how *Mami* and her
cousin, *Titi Argelia,* tried to console her it didn't work. For
nine days after he was buried they had a novena, where the
family gathered together to say the rosary and pray for *Tio
Guillo's* soul. Each night, by the third repetition of *Santa
María, Madre de Diós* (Sainted Mary, mother of God) *Titi
Juana-Inez* sobbed inconsolably. She was so dramatic it made
me cry too. That was the thing about living above the funeral
parlor, there were a lot of tears and sadness. At times like
this I wondered how much longer we would live above there.

I was four years old when my baby sister Venus arrived,
and the harmony and routine of my life changed. I became
my mother's assistant, a job I would have for a very long time.
My time spent staring at the mourners came to a halt. At
first I loved watching and holding baby Venus. She was so
cute, a perfect miniature live doll with toes and hands
making gurgling noises. But soon I was given my first big
sister job, washing her dirty diapers. Every day *Mami* would
fill up the bathtub with at least a dozen stinky diapers and
give me the washboard so I could scrub the brown and green
poop stains out of them. I couldn't believe how formula and
baby food could stink so much and would put a wooden
clothespin on my nose during this smelly task.

It was a small apartment with only one bedroom, so I
slept in the living room sofa daybed and Venus slept in her
crib in *Mami* and *Papito's* room. Poor baby, she didn't get to
sleep in the bureau drawer like I did. Now they were so
taken up with their love child—that's what they called
Venus—they didn't play or read with me as much. I
entertained myself by playing on the floor in the closet or
gazing out the window at the mourners.

About six months after Venus arrived, I had a dream
that I got up in the middle of the night and went to the
bathroom. When I woke up the next morning my bed was
soaking wet. *Mami* was very angry. She scolded me and made
me scrub the mattress real hard to get the stain and the

stink out. Then we flipped the mattress over and put a plastic cover underneath the sheets.

One night, a week or so later, as I dreamt that I was in the bathroom peeing, I was awakened by a dark figure dressed in black with a big hooked nose and wearing a tall pointy hat like a witch. The witch scooped me up and yelled at me, "You bad girl, you've peed in the bed again." I began to wail like the mourners. The witch twirled me around in her arms, shook me and threw me onto the bed where *Papito* was. He took me from the witch and hugged and soothed me until I calmed down.

Mami came into the room and *Papito* said, *"tu estas loca Dina*—are you crazy?" *"Bueno,* I had to find some way to make her stop peeing in her sleep," she responded still laughing like a witch. I realized then that the witch had been *Mami* and started to cry all over again. "I'm sorry, *Mijita,"* she said patting my curls, "but I just had to do something."

I hated this place. Ever since my first scary visit there was were always sad people, dead people, and now witches. "I want to move from here, *Papito*, take me away. I promise to stop peeing in bed if you promise to move out of the funeral parlor before next Halloween." In fact, after that night I never peed in my bed again and every day I kept asking *Mami* and *Papito*, "When are we moving, when?" I was like a broken record asking the same question again and again.

2

FROM EL BARRIO TO EL BRONX

By the summer of 1951, Venus was two years old, able to walk and getting very feisty. She was getting too big to share *Mami* and *Papito*'s bedroom and we rarely had company because the living room was my bedroom. It was clear that our small, one bedroom apartment over the funeral parlor was just too cramped for the four of us.

For weeks and weeks, *Mami* and *Papito* spent Sunday afternoons looking at apartments where we lived in Manhattan's *El Barrio* (East Harlem), in Brooklyn, where my cousin Gladys lived, and in The Bronx. During these apartment-hunting trips, *Abuela* took care of Venus and me, and *Abuelo* looked after the funeral parlor. This was hard for him when we had English speaking customers because *Abuelo* only spoke Spanish, so I often ended up being his helper.

At long last it was time to move and get as far away as possible from the dreary sad funeral parlor I hated so much; I was done with dead people and their crying families. *Mami* and *Papito* found a nine-room apartment in the South Bronx where *Papito* was to be the superintendent. And the best part was that *Abuelita* and *Abuelo* were going to move with us just as I'd always dreamed. We were all going to live together in one big place and save money. *Abuelita* would take care of us and cook her delicious food everyday and I could sit and listen to *Abuelo*'s storytelling while *Mami* and *Papito* were at work.

Venus didn't seem to be too happy about this change, so she took it out on me on moving day by throwing my *Doña Missy* out of the front window. *Doña Missy* had a Raggedy Ann-type body made of cloth, but her face was made of plaster. When Missy hit the sidewalk on her way down the front steps of our building, her head crashed and splintered into smithereens. I was so angry with Venus I pulled her hair until she cried. *Papito* stopped in the middle of moving and patiently picked up all the pieces of Missy's face, promising to put her back together for me. Every night the first week in our brand new big apartment, *Papito* patiently glued Missy's face together piece by piece, but she never looked the same. Missy now had lots of lines on her face that made her look like a wrinkled old lady and her eyes looked as if she were frozen in fright. I hugged and kissed Missy each night and cried myself to sleep with her next to me for months.

We moved from *El Barrio* to *El Bronx* into a five-story brick apartment building with a fancy entrance. I remember entering 748 Beck Street for the first time through the main entrance that had two heavy wrought-iron and glass doors leading into a small hallway that led to a second set of glass doors covered with lace curtains. On the right were shiny brass mailboxes, with ivory-colored buttons on the bottom which you pressed, and then someone upstairs buzzed you in. *Papito*'s name, *P. Castaño,* was already on our mailbox and underneath it was *Abuelo* and *Abuelita*'s last name, *Santiago-Gouglas* insisted on using both his last names, especially since his mother's maiden name was French.

Once I passed the second set of doors it was simply a hallway that smelled a little musty with stairs and tiled floors that weren't too clean. There were two apartment doors on each floor and when we entered our apartment door with the number four painted in gold, everything was dark, mysterious and immaculate. *Abuelo*'s brothers, my grand uncles, *Tio Guillo* and *Tio Valentin,* lived upstairs with their sister *Titi María,* who was a widow. They were all single. Well sort of. I soon learned *Titi* was in fact permanently separated and never divorced as that was unheard of those days. It seems her husband had committed an "indiscretion with one of those women," so she kicked him out of the house and told everyone he was dead. No one ever explained to me what an "indiscretion" was, though I later looked the word up in the dictionary, which didn't tell much more.

Both *Tio Valentín* and *Tio Guillo* always dressed in tailored suits that fit perfectly. They wore spats on their shoes, and hats that made them look very dapper. *Tio Valentin* liked the white straw hat with the black ribbon around it, and *Tio Guillo* liked the felt fedora hats where the brim covered his face and made him look mysterious, like a detective. He was very handsome with dark chocolate skin and black, tightly waved, shiny hair slicked down with *Brilliantina* pomade. *Titi María* always dressed in her Sunday best as if she were going to church every day, which she did.

I entered our apartment by way of a lovely foyer, then made a sharp right turn into the living room. Off the living room was a bedroom with two French doors, the ones with lots of little glass panes that slide into a crevice in the doorframe and became part of the wall. This is the room *Mami* and *Papito* chose for themselves. Straight in front of us was a long hallway, but we had to go through the dining room first. As I continued on down the hallway, there were a number of rooms all on the right side: first was the kitchen, then the bathroom. Next, there were two small bedrooms, each with a window and a fire escape: the first was for *Abuela* and *Abuelo*, the second was to be shared between Venus and me. What a disappointment! The last room, the biggest, was to become "the rental suite." What was the purpose of moving to a bigger place if I still couldn't have my own room and why did we have to live with people we didn't even know? Oh well, it was still a zillion times better than living over a funeral parlor, that's for sure.

Except for the fact that it was in a five-story building, it felt like we had moved into a house. Even our Godmother Delis' house in New Jersey wasn't this big. The dining room and living room walls were painted a deep forest green, accented with white trim and ceilings. Everywhere I went, people painted the walls white, pure white or linen white, but always white. Here, there was this deep dark forest green color and I loved it. It was kind of mysterious like the homes I read about it books, and though it was dark, I found it warm and inviting. It reminded me of the smell of pine trees, like having Christmas all year long. The foyer had this wonderful wallpaper with oodles of dark green leaves and vines against a white backdrop on the top half, separated by a trim in the middle, called wainscoting, and the bottom half was the same forest green that was in the dining room. The leaves looked as if they had been hand-painted. The foyer also held a beautiful piece of furniture that I fell in love with the moment I saw it. It was a combination bookshelf with glass doors on top, a desk in the middle, and three drawers underneath. An old-fashioned silver key unlocked the slanted wooden flap that formed a desktop when opened, revealing little shelves and tiny drawers. To the right of this desk was a small chair made of the same dark mahogany wood, and above it was a black wall phone like in the old black and white movies of the twenties, thirties, and forties. I felt sure they were all antiques. Throughout most of the apartment the floors were covered with linoleum in a pale sage-green pattern of flowing leaves that looked like feathery fans, except in the kitchen where the linoleum was sepia-toned.

The grand green dining room is where the family usually congregated because it was next to the kitchen. It had a dark wooden rectangular table covered with a lovely white linen embroidered table cloth and was surrounded by ten high-backed chairs. There were three important pieces of furniture in this room as well. A tall cabinet with shelves between the two windows that faced the interior courtyard and the dining room table with eight high-backed chairs. But, the most important piece of furniture in this room, in fact in the entire house, at least as far as Venus and I were concerned, was an old-fashioned, intricately carved, heavy dark wooden upright, which we immediately baptized *El Piano*.

Our rent was ninety dollars a month. Can you imagine? That's ten dollars per room! It probably costs two thousand dollars or more today, that is, if it hasn't been broken up into two or three apartments at one thousand dollars each. We lived there for ten years and even after all that time the rent was still a bargain at $180 a month. That's because my father was *El Super* for the building.

The owner of the building, Mr. Catalano, always said that *Papito* was the best superintendent he'd ever hired, even years after we'd moved out. It's true! *Papito* knew how to fix everything and he kept the hallways spic-n-span clean. He painted the walls, polished the mailboxes and repaired anything that broke in the apartments. He made closets and cabinets, painted the building hallway in two tones like our foyer. On the top half he used a pale green color like the tropical ocean, which everyone in the building loved, and for the bottom half he used the dark green, because he had so much of that color in the basement. He separated the two colors with a stenciled pattern that was very popular in the fifties. And in no time flat, he'd gotten rid of that musty smell that had greeted us the day we moved in.

Papito fancied himself quite the interior decorator. After being in our apartment for a year, he started to redecorate, beginning with the kitchen. He decided that since we spent so much time in the dining room he'd connect the kitchen and dining room by making a hole in the wall. He designed a countertop bar with stools on each side, like in my favorite soda shop. Over the bar he built a cabinet that held beautiful crystal jars and goblets that *Mami* and *Abuelita* found in the secondhand shops for pennies. Connecting these two rooms was a great idea because whoever was in the kitchen preparing meals could talk with those in the dining room. It also made it easier for *Mami* to supervise our homework and study time while she cooked, or, better said, helped *Abuela* cook. I loved the idea of all the women in the house being together as if it were our own special quiet time.

Papito's next project was to design and build a linen closet for the very small bathroom in our very big apartment. With nine people in the apartment we needed storage space, so *Papito* built a closet in the long hallway right outside of the bathroom. The living room was next and here *Papito* went all out. He painted the walls a pale linen peachy color and made the window trim look like wood by painting nodules into the trim then shellacking it to give it a nice sheen. He also sanded the floor and stained it the same color as the woodwork trim.

In the living room, *Papito* put up a wallpaper mural on the far end wall of a tropical panoramic scene with a lake and palm trees, from the Florida Everglades that reminded the elders of the lushness and warmth of Puerto Rico and Cuba. The neighbors thought *Papito* was talented and creative because he made our house look unique. I agree. He was a very talented craftsman. It was his pride and joy and it became my dream house.

I have a classic photograph of the family sitting in the Florida Room in front of that mural on Christmas in 1956. Was dressed up in a satin maroon and gray patterned smoking jacket, holding his pipe. *Mami* sat proudly at his side wearing her sexy black dress with the sweetheart collar accented by rhinestone pendants on each corner. *Papito* loved that dress. Actually, what he loved was *Mami*'s cleavage, but he always complimented the dress and how *bella* she looked in it. Venus and I sat at their feet wearing the shiny pale blue-green dresses with fur collars and matching muffs that our Godmother Delis had given us that year. Next to us sat our majestic collie, Sabu, and perfectly placed in the background so that it didn't hide the mural, was our beautifully decorated Christmas tree. That is the room where we had special events, received our guests and where oftentimes *Papito* gave his lectures—*Abuelo* called them *tertulias*.

Papito always had a project going on in the apartment. I remember he once decided he wanted a stereo set with all the bells and whistles so he could listen to the big band music and salsa records he loved. He had albums from the best Cuban musicians. One of his favorites was the classical Cuban composer Ernesto Lecuona, and his and *Mami*'s favorite bolero singer was Lucho Gatica, whose voice was sultry and romantic. *Papito* also loved The 1001 Strings and he collected all of the albums. The speakers he wanted were so expensive that he decided to build them himself. He could only work on the speakers during the weekends, which drove *Mami* crazy because that's when she wanted his undivided attention, so we nicknamed it "the never-ending project." *Mami* and I took turns reading the instructions out loud in English first so we could understand them, and then translating them so he could build it, bit by bit. It was worth it though, because when they were finally complete, it sounded as if the 1001 strings were playing live in our living room.

Papito's tertulias were usually about politics, especially the situation in Puerto Rico and Cuba. He'd talk about the Spanish-American War and how Cuba and Puerto Rico were related to the U.S., and about how slavery, poverty and the political struggles on both islands had a lot in common. He

spoke about men like Jose Marti, Cuba's most revered and
prolific poet, writer and visionary, and about Pedro Albizu-
Campos, Puerto Rico's nationalist orator. Both were men of
vision who loved their country and fought to rid their
homelands of slavery and imperialist control. Eventually he
began talking about Fidel Castro and the impending
revolution that he believed would erupt in Cuba. Few people
believed it would ever come to pass. But, when Castro finally
ousted the dictator Fulgencio Battista from Cuba in 1959,
Papito was the only pro-Castro Cuban we knew at that time,
and because of his opinions, many of his Cuban friends
distanced themselves from him.

The best thing about moving to Beck Street, aside from
getting out of that dreary funeral parlor, was that our family
became very big. We saw each other every day, and almost
always ate the evening meal together. Living in this
extended family environment was wonderful most of the
time and soon our neighbors would become family as well.

3

NINE ROOMS AND ONE TINY BATHROOM!

Titi María and *Abuela* were excellent cooks, which was a blessing for *Mami*, who wasn't too good in the kitchen. Another good thing is that there was always someone around and there was lots of conversation and laughter. But, there was a downside to this living arrangement. I never had privacy. And worse yet, we ended up having to explain everything to each person, over and over again, first in English to *Mami* so we could practice, and then again in Spanish to our elders and yet again to our tenants. Any time Venus or I did something wrong, like get home late from school or get a bad report card or were seen talking to the wrong kids, there was this unending litany of reprimands from every member of the family, blood relative or not. Throughout the day or the week, one by one each adult would make a comment or ask a question about your latest mistake. One by one they'd ask us, "*Cuentame*. Tell me what happened with your report card" or "I heard you got home late from

school today, *por que,* why?" And over and over again you had
to courteously explain: what a drag!

   Papito worked the night shift in a downtown building,
and came home at about eleven nightly. M*ami* felt it was
really important for us to see *Papito,* so at least once a week
she would make us take a nap between eight and ten and
then wake us up for a couple of hours so we could visit with
him. It was great fun. *Papito* would come home, take his
shower, then eat while we kept him company telling him
about our friends, school, daily activities, and yes, indiscretions
too. It was always best if we told him first so he'd get our
version before he got *Mami*'s version, which was always a little
more exaggerated. After that he'd get in bed and *Mami*
would cradle his head on her bosom and talk to him while
Venus massaged his feet and I combed the hairs on his chest
and made pin curls with bobby pins. Of course, the next
morning it was really hard getting out of bed for school, but
we managed. That's why we only did this once a week.

   It's funny about *Mami,* she really wasn't the world's best
housewife, which is the way people used to measure the
quality or ability of "motherhood" in those days. Could she
cook? Was her house immaculate and her children clean?
Well, the fact is *Mami* didn't rate too well in these categories,
yet in other ways she was absolutely great. She was intricately
involved in our school lessons and activities. I mean *Mami*
was dead serious about our reading and doing our homework.
She also made sure we got some outdoor exercise every day
unless it was bitter cold. I know that's when she took her
nap so she could be fresh and lovely for *Papito* when he came
home. For an hour, Venus and I were on our own outdoors
right underneath the living room window breathing in some
fresh South Bronx City air. She took us to museums and
artistic events, like plays and the ballet, which I loved. We
often went to The Cloisters or ice skating in Central Park.
Venus hated all of this stuff but I lapped it up. Most important

of all, she taught us to have dreams and goals. She encouraged my sister's piano playing and my singing, and made sure we did some of this every day after being outdoors. *Mami* encouraged me to sing and try out for the Star Search program on WNYC, the New York City municipal radio station. When I was selected as one of the participants from about fifty kids, there was a little celebration waiting at home. *Mami* even baked a cake. It was lopsided but delicious. Once a month on Saturdays at 9 a.m., I'd go the station and sing a couple of romantic songs and the entire family would listen in. This made *Mami* beam with pleasure and I basked in her joy.

She was also very involved in our education. School was serious business, no lateness or missed classes, unless we were deathly ill; and no failing grades either. At the time *Mami* was the only Puerto Rican mother who attended the PTA meetings, mostly because she didn't work outside the home like the other mothers did, and also because she spoke English very well. She made it her business to keep the other mothers informed on the issues.

But, as a housewife, *Mami* couldn't cut it. With the exception of *Papito*'s two favorite dishes, Cuban black beans and *picadillo*, savory ground meat with tomato sauce, olives and raisins, her cooking left a lot to be desired. Actually, she could clean up a storm if she wanted to, but she rarely did because she hated it. So guess who did it? Me! In the beginning I didn't mind, though it was hard work and took up most of Saturday morning and afternoon, but as time went on I began to resent the fact that only *Abuela* and I seemed to have that responsibility. I mean, what was I—her maid or her daughter? I loved Mami because she encouraged my dreams and cared about school, but I resented being her back-up housewife.

Mami was also hot-tempered. She took a long time to flare up, but when she did, watch out. If she had something in her hands, a book, a pot, the phone, it's as if the heat of

her temper made the object fly out of her hands right in
the direction of whoever was in her way. In those days students
in public school came home for lunch and we had an hour
to walk home, eat, then walk back to school. I remember
one day they let us out fifteen minutes later than usual,
meaning I only had forty-five minutes to get home eat and
return to school. I gulped my lunch and as I was leaving
Mami asked me to take down the garbage, which meant I'd
have to go to the basement and come back upstairs with the
garbage can. "But, Mami I'll be late for school and you hate
that." The next thing I knew the *cacerola* she was washing
came flying at me from the kitchen through the dining room
into the foyer. Fortunately I ducked. So, I took the garbage
down, raced back upstairs, then flew to school, barely making
it in before the doors were locked. *Papito* cajoled and
pleaded with *Mami* to get her out of this habit, but it never
took; though she did it less and less. Whenever he needed
to have a serious talk with her, he'd go up to her, gently take
whatever she had in her hands away and place it out of her
reach. Then, while firmly holding onto her hands, he spoke
softly to her as if he were telling a story. The funny thing is
Mami always managed to slip a hand away and pick up
another object and the minute she got angry, zoom, it would
go flying in the air. She broke one of two beautiful black
jaguar figurines we had on the living room coffee table
because *Papi Angel* hadn't sent the monthly money order as
promised. Another time she totaled the receiver of our old-
fashioned heavy black telephone. It got so we avoided having
too many *chachka*s around the house.

    Mami was good at organizing things. The one room that
was a bone of contention for everyone in our apartment was
the bathroom. After all, there were nine people living in
this big, five-bedroom apartment: two people in three of
the rooms, plus our two tenants and one teeny tiny bathroom
for all of us to use everyday, morning, noon, night and in-
between. *El maldito baño* was the cause of many logistical

frustrations for our extended family, so *Mami* devised a schedule for us. The adults who went to work early, like *Papito* and Sylvia, showered and shaved in the morning at specific times. Venus, *Mami* and I bathed at night before going to bed as did *Abuela*, who believed it helped her sleep better. I later learned most Puerto Ricans do this, because on the Island you sweat all day and want to go to bed nice and fresh. *Abuelo* usually woke up around mid-day, by which time most of us were gone, so he could have the bathroom whenever he wanted and usually for as long as he wanted.

I've never understood why the most-used room in the house is the smallest. If I were to design an apartment or a home the bathroom would definitely be the biggest room. After all, it's where you brush your teeth, bathe, shave, put on your make-up and sit on the throne. *Abuelo* read the newspaper everyday while sitting on the throne. If I were an architect, I'd separate the bathroom into two sections. I'd put the sink and the toilet bowl in one room, and a sink and a bathtub with a shower in another room. Now that makes sense. Years later, on my first trip to Europe, I discovered that is exactly how they did it, one room for the throne and another for washing and shaving. Very sensible!

Here is another place where *Papito*'s handy work saved the day. He built a great closet in the hall right outside of the bathroom, which held all the toiletries and linens. Every room had two shelves, with their own label. Even Sabu had a little shelf. At the very bottom was *Papito*'s tool chest, with a bilingual sign that read, "Don't touch my tools—*no toquen mis tools.*" He was very particular about all of his things. He had signs like that all over the house, even in his drawers. These were primarily for *Mami*, because she'd used his things and never put them back in place. She, of course, ignored these signs and called him a *majadero* meaning "finicky."

They constantly argued about the scissors. *Papito* had these small delicate scissors for trimming his mustache and the hairs in his nose. Whenever *Mami* needed a pair of scissors, instead of using the pair *Papito* bought her, she'd go into his drawer and use his tiny delicate grooming scissors. Inevitably he'd go to use them and they were either not where he always placed them, or worse, they'd be dull and that's when their argument would begin.

"*Dina, querida, amor mio,*" he'd start. "My darling, dearest sweetheart, why do you always use my scissors?" he'd say in his smooth and loving Ricky Ricardo-accented voice. "You know these are delicate instruments and have to be perfect to trim my *biogote*. That's why I bought you your own pair, please use them, *querida.*"

"*Hay Nene,*" she'd respond, "you're such a pain, *que mucho fastidias!*"

Then she'd promise not to use them and give him a smoochy kiss on his lips. He'd sigh deeply and smile at her adoringly. But a few weeks later she'd use his special scissors again and this scene would repeat itself, like a hit tune or a commercial on the radio. At about the fourth time *Mami* used the special scissors, *Papito* would get really angry and they'd argue at the top of the lungs like Lucy and Ricky. By nighttime, though, they'd kiss and make up. They had a special rule, and that was to never go to bed angry.

Mami also organized a rotating schedule for cleaning the bathroom. Each of us was assigned a week, which took care of the month. Twice a week, the tub and bowl were scrubbed, the floor mopped, and the hand towels changed. We each had different colored towels and kept them in our bedrooms since there wasn't enough space in the bathroom, and besides, it would have been too confusing to keep track of all those towels. What both amazed and pissed me off, because it was unfair and made me feel like the "Cinderella" of the household, is that *Mami* and my lazy sister Venus managed to almost never have to clean the bathroom.

This bathroom schedule seemed to work out fine until my older brother Angel Jr. came to spend the summers with us. He acted as if the bathroom was his private space for grooming and crooning to his rock-n-roll songs. He spent more time in front of the mirror than any of the women in the house, shaving, picking his pimples, combing his Frankie Avalon pompadour, and singing at himself adoringly as if he were on stage with a microphone. He'd stand in front of the sink and mirror, spread his legs out, tilt his hips in like Elvis Presley and stroke his hair over and over again. I tell you, the man, excuse me, the boy, loved himself. It was always a battle to get him out of there.

Abuelo was the other one who took forever with his special rituals. Besides sitting on the throne for an hour every day, patiently reading *El Diario*, he'd be in the bathroom twice a week, shaving his head and his beard. He'd fill the sink with steaming hot water, then make his foamy soap mixture in a small bowl. Then he'd lather himself up like Santa Claus, all the while making funny faces *muecas* in the mirror. Slowly and carefully while stroking his chin, cheeks and neck with the razor, he'd twist his lips to the left, then to the right and squint at himself while jutting his chin upwards, and puckered his lips out like a fish, which always made me giggle. I sometimes think he did it with that purpose in mind.

The kitchen was the other room that got cleaned a lot. Every night after the last meal, *Mami* washed the dishes— the one chore she always did and she did it well, while I cleaned the stove and counter tops and mopped the floor. *Mami* had it really good with two live-in maids. One cooked, the other one cleaned; no wonder she liked the extended family set-up. I sometimes felt like "Cinderella" always doing housework and cleaning and wondered how *Abuela* felt always being in the kitchen, but she never made a smirk nor complained nor said a word to me about it.

My parents' room held a special appeal for Venus and me. There was something almost mysterious about it, which of course made us very curious. It had this unique sweet pungent odor—a blend of *Mami*'s perfume, *La Habanera*, *Papito*'s Old Spice after-shave lotion, and I believe, their own essence. The night tables on each side were always stacked with books or magazines and their bed had lots of comfy pillows at the headboard so you could sit up to read. *Mami* and *Papito* both loved to read and spent a lot of time alone together in their room. It's where they had their quiet time, whispering gently and romantically, while Venus and I listened from the dining room straining to hear their conversations. We couldn't really make out what they said, but loved the tone of their affectionate chats. *"Hay Pedrito,"* *Mami* would say, to which *Papito* would reply, *"Que mi nena,* what, my sweetheart?" They never argued or fought in that room. They just made lots of gushy and moaning-like noises. Arguments and discussions took place in the living room, the kitchen or dining room, but never in their bedroom. Some nights, when *Papito* got home early from work, all four of us would sit on the bed and talk or play, and oftentimes they would read to us. No one ever interrupted us there, I guess because it was our sacred place.

Since they didn't have a lot of money to go out to dance clubs, on weekends *Mami* and *Papito* played romantic music and danced *boleros* swaying and holding onto each other tightly, creating beautiful shadows in the candlelit room. That's probably why the rest of us spent so much time in the dining room because the living room was like their private space. Even though Venus and I knew this was another way for them to keep tabs on us, we never stopped trying to outsmart them and sneak out. Of course, we also never succeeded because no matter how romantically distracted they were, their radar was always in tip-top condition when it came to us.

Television viewing was usually a family affair. *Mami* believed that kids had to play outside at least a half-hour everyday, no matter how cold. The only time we didn't have to play outside was if it rained. Of course, if it snowed we couldn't wait to get outside and begged to stay until it was dark. If we hadn't played outside and completed our homework, we were not allowed to watch TV, and when we were permitted to watch, it was a specifically approved program. *Abuelo* and *Abuela* preferred to go to their room and listen to the *novelas* on the radio, except when the *I Love Lucy* show with Lucille Ball and her Cuban husband, Desi Arnaz, came on. We all loved that program and so did all our neighbors in the building and most of our friends. Aside from the fact that they were hysterical and made us all laugh uncontrollably, especially me, it was the only place on television where I saw someone like *Papito*—a *Cubano*, a *Latino*. *Desi's* accent was just like *Papito's* and he also always said *pero chico* this and *pero chica* that, and exclaimed *alabao* whenever he forgot something. But, it was my favorite because Lucy and Desi reminded me of *Mami* and *Papito's* constant and funny bickering, like when they argued over his mustache scissors.

We celebrated many wonderful Christmas and New Year's Eve holidays and rituals in that living room. Whether it was trimming the tree with new decorations made by each member of the family or writing our gift list. Of course, it was a short list. We were only allowed to ask for two things: one personal wish-type thing, like passing my math exams— I was terrible at math—and one special present, something you really truly wanted, like ice skates, a phonograph, or a Barbie doll with glasses. And, we were each expected to make a wish for those people who were in trouble or had less than we did.

Another favorite ritual, that Venus and I adored was the one we performed on New Year's Eve. After we were all dressed up and packed for our overnight party excursion, we'd drink champagne and eat twelve green grapes, one for every month of the year. As we ate each grape we'd make a personal wish and take a sip of our champagne. Actually, Venus and I had *Cidra* sparking cider, which had bubbles and looked like champagne in the glass. We didn't get real champagne until we were sixteen. This was a tradition that

Papito and his family in Cuba practiced. It was our very special family ritual, *Mami, Papito,* Venus and I, and of course, our collie, Sabu, who always watched whatever we did with great curious wonder. He'd look from one to the other, alternately raising an eyebrow, perhaps wondering if he was going to get grapes too. Once I gave him one and he spat it out. Not sweet enough for his taste, I guess. I relished this ritual and planned out my wishes very carefully each year, one for each member of the family, one for the less fortunate in the world, and the rest for myself. My wishes always centered on my singing. I always prayed that *Abuela* would keep winning at *la bolita* (the lottery numbers game) so I could keep taking voice and ballet lessons and that I'd get discovered like Lana Turner did. Then I could be on television with Desi and Lucy and make lots of money, so I could buy a big family home. That was at least until I fell in love and then made wishes about my sweetheart.

Right after the champagne and the wishing-grapes, we'd leave for the New Year's Eve party, and I do mean party. Each year the party would take place at the home of one of the three families: my godmother Delis and her daughter Delita's home, another Cuban friend of *Papito*'s, Orestes, his wife Eugenia and their three kids, Ginny, Pepe and Roberto and our home. Roberto had copper red hair, which I'd never seen on a guy, and lots of freckles. He was super smart and good in every subject, but he was so shy he could barely talk to anyone, except me, that is. We were good friends and he helped me with my math. We'd usually sit in his room for an hour, while the party was getting underway and just talk about books and music. We both loved The Platters and hated Elvis Presley. Each family would contribute something to make an incredible feast of Cuban and Puerto Rican food: *pasteles, arroz con gandules, lechon asado,* and a salad of lettuce, tomatoes, watercress, purple onions and avocado. There were also delicious desserts: *dulce de leche* (sweet milk curd) and guava paste with white cheese called *queso del pais, Papito*'s favorite dessert.

We'd arrive, hug and kiss everyone at least three or four times, and get busy setting up the food area. Then it was time to dance, dance, dance. It was the only time that *Mami* and *Papito* ever drank cocktails. *Mami* would have champagne and *Papito* would have his *Cuba Libre*, rum and Coke with lime. That's why we'd stay over until the next morning. We'd sleep all over the house, kids in one room, adults in the others, then wake up about mid-morning, have a huge breakfast, help clean up the house, and go home and sleep some more.

Once, I remember my sister and I sneaked into the kitchen and drank up all the unfinished liquid in the empty glasses that were on the kitchen counter. We got a little tipsy and danced around in circles in the middle of the floor until Venus got dizzy and threw up. It's a miracle we didn't get spanked and punished. *Mami, Papito, Los Abuelos* and *Titi María* were quite strict. There were lots of rules and when they were broken, we'd know about it. There usually was a spanking from *Mami*, recriminations from everyone else in the family, and the final reprimand from *Papito* when he was told of the incident. Though they weren't practicing Catholics, meaning they didn't go to Church every Sunday, though I was required to, we pretty much obeyed the Ten Commandments. No lying, no cheating, no disrespecting the adults, and so forth. But, on that evening there was no scolding or spanking, I guess, because it was a childish prank and everyone was having fun, three generations of three families dancing up a storm and enjoying each other totally.

When we had the party at our house, it was the best. Daddy would turn on the make-believe fireplace he'd made that reflected wonderful amber-colored patterns on the walls, dim the lights and make it romantic, and we'd all dance till dawn. It was the only time I didn't have to help with the cleaning up because the grown-ups did all the work, while the kids played games. Sometimes we'd end the evening with Venus playing *El Piano* while I led all of us singing *villancicos* (Christmas carols) in Spanish, like *"Alegria, Alegria, Alegria"* or *"Pastores A Belen."*

The room in which there was a great deal of arguing was the one I shared with my darling not-too-neat younger sister. There was an invisible wall in the middle of this small rectangular, cramped room that contained one dresser and two beds separated by one night table. We also shared the one closet and one window, both on Venus's side of the room, of course. My side was neat, clean and orderly and Venus's side always looked like a disaster area. She never made her bed and always had a pile of things on top of it—clothes, shoes, towels, books, toys, whatever. During the daytime the pile was on her bed, at nighttime she dumped it on the floor at the foot of her bed. The next morning she'd sort of make her bed by pulling up the bedspread over the pillow, and then dumping the pile from the floor back onto the foot of her bed. This routine would go on for weeks until *Mami* couldn't stand it any longer, which was always bad for me because I ended up having to clean both sides of our room. You see, Venus was *La Nena Linda*, the pretty girl of the house, which means she was spoiled and almost always got her way. She rarely did housework or ran errands or washed the dishes, which I resented. Why should I have to do more just because she's pretty or was it because I was the half-sister? But, even though she made me mad and at times drove me nuts, I loved her too, so I also spoiled her and let her get away with a lot of stuff just like my parents did.

Our tenant, Sylvia, was a crazy, hot-blooded, sexy, loud, gregarious, warm, loving, funny *Cubanita*, which means she and *Papito* had a lot in common. She flirted with *Papito* all the time, which made Venus furious. *Mami* was so secure about having *Papito* wrapped around her little finger she didn't pay much attention to Sylvia's shenanigans, but Venus was very possessive of *Papito*. It's bad enough she had to share him with me, but with an outsider, that was the limit. Venus always made sure she sat between Sylvia and *Papito* so she couldn't touch him when they talked. In fact, she never really did anything but flirt, just to tease Venus, I think. As far as I was concerned, Sylvia couldn't hold a candle to my mother. *Mami* was sultry, zaftig, intelligent, understated and graceful, whereas Sylvia was loud, pushy and clumsy. *Papito* didn't like loud and pushy, he liked mysterious and intelligent. So, even though *Mami* couldn't cook, *Papito* was totally smitten by her. Actually, *Mami* was pretty smart, she learned how to cook three things perfectly, all *Papito*'s favorite dishes, of course. She made excellent Cuban black beans, *yucca con mojo* (yucca pan fried in garlic and olive oil with lemon juice) and *picadillo*, a Cuban staple. She really didn't need to know how to make anything else because *Papito* would happily eat this stuff every day practically.

Mami's cooking nemesis, however, was the most important staple of Cuban and Puerto Rican food. Rice! She just never got it right. It was either too soft, *amogollao*, or it was *quemao*, practically burnt. So, I made the rice and I made it perfectly every time. We were quite a team, *Mami* and I; we took care of *Papito*'s stomach just right.

Marta, our second tenant, was also Cuban. She was tall, shy and regal looking, like I imagined an African Queen would look and walk. She wasn't pretty or beautiful but she was smart, strong and serene. Marta and *Papito* had the same political perspective on Cuba, whereas Sylvia was totally anti-Castro. Marta could see the inevitability of the Cuban revolution as well as the benefits that Castro brought. She proudly cited his primary goal, a program to educate all of the children on the island, especially the poor and black children, called *alfabetización*.

Whenever Sylvia and Marta were together, they argued a lot. Sylvia was gregarious and a little vulgar. She often cursed and told jokes, to which *Mami* ascribed one of her fancy words, saying they were *risqué*. In contrast, Marta was serious, quiet and reserved. But they both had three important things in common: they were single females, hard working and

Cuban, like *Papito*. Deep down, they really liked each other, but took pleasure in the bickering and the debates.

Eventually, Marta met and fell in love with Mike, a Greek guy she met in English class. She only spoke Spanish, he spoke Greek, yet in spite of the language difficulties, which I think says a lot about love crossing all borders, they got married before they totally spoke English. I guess there are times in a relationship where words are not necessary, and those are probably the times when it didn't matter. They had the emotion. It was wonderful watching the two of them talking to each other, and I especially liked being their interpreter. I didn't speak Greek, but I did speak Spanish and English. Mike was better at speaking English because he had been studying it longer than Marta. Our form of communication was that Marta talked to me in Spanish and then I would translate it for Mike in English and he would respond in English-Greek, often using his hands in body language. We used to laugh a lot during these sessions but always in a loving and respectful way. Mr. and Mrs. Petrakis lived with us for a couple of years until they saved enough money and knew enough English to be on their own and moved to a cute place in Brooklyn. Then Paíto and Carmenlina, also Cubans, moved in and stayed a long time, and their first child, Thalia, was born at 748 Beck Street. Running from the cold, Thalia's family eventually moved to Florida. I'm sorry to say I've lost track of Marta, Mike and Sylvia; for years I tried to find them but was unsuccessful.

Mami and I used to be the English teachers at home. Twice a week, we'd have English reading sessions with Marta, Mike, Sylvia and *Papito*. It was great practice for me and ended up being helpful with my English at school, but it had the opposite effect on my Spanish. Between teachers insisting that we're in America now and here we speak English and Spanish-speaking people at home wanting to learn English, I began forgetting my Spanish. So, in high school I decided to take Spanish as my language elective. It was frustrating trying to learn Spanish from a teacher who taught it with an American accent. Ms. Vogel always insisted that I pronounce Spanish her way, with a North American accent, instead of my way, the correct way with a Spanish accent. Go figure! The good news is that I learned English and I didn't forget my Spanish. In fact, I got a ninety-nine on the statewide Regents exam and since I was weak in math, especially algebra, this helped keep up my overall average, which was important if I was going to get into college. More to the point, I loved being able to speak, read and write in two languages and being able to say that I was bilingual!

Living with the eight people in my extended bilingual family had its ups and downs and was a constant challenge. But mostly, it was great fun and it wasn't boring. We shared traditions and rituals and stories from Puerto Rico, Cuba, the Bronx and the U.S., and there was an abundance of laughter, love and people to share it all with.

4

FACES AND PLACES IN THE HOOD

The front stoop at 748 Beck Street was one of my favorite places, the absolute best being the windowsill in our living room, because from there I could see for two or three blocks in any direction. It was very entertaining.

But I spent a lot of time on the stoop reading, playing jacks by myself or jumping rope and hopscotch with my girlfriends. During our daily outside excursions, we were never allowed to go beyond that quarter of the block between my stoop and the corner of 156th Street without permission. That way *Mami* and *Abuelita*, or anyone else in the family, could check up on us at any time, and believe you me they did. I never knew when *Mami* or *Abuelita* were going to call from the window yelling *Mija*, that meant me, "go to the *bodega* and buy some *leche y pan*." Running errands to the *bodega* to get milk and bread was a daily ritual, and if I wasn't right there on the front stoop or in that quarter of the block there was trouble to be had.

Not only was my family large, but the entire building was

an extended family. The good part of this is that the kids all played together and ran in and out of each other's homes munching our way through every kitchen, making noise and playing with each other's toys. The bad part was that, if you did something wrong or got in trouble, everybody knew about it and each and every one had something to say about it. The litany of reprimands was long, repetitive and tedious.

One of my best childhood girlfriends, Brenda Rhonda, lived next door in Apartment 3. We were the same age and very close. Her last name reminded me of a lovely song titled *Noche de Ronda*, which means "nighttime wandering." Brenda and I walked to and from school, did our homework and played pick-up sticks and jacks on the stoop together almost every day. She lived in the nine-room apartment next door with her mother and father, *Doña Fela*, a seamstress and housewife, and *Don Efraín*, who made and repaired guitars and violins. Actually, they had another daughter, Adriana, who was fifteen years older than Brenda and married with kids, who visited them at least once a month.

In contrast to *Mami*, *Doña Fela* kept the most meticulous house I'd ever seen; everything always looked new and shiny and inviting. She always set the table for dinner and lit candles. Like *Mami* and *Papito*, they were a romantic couple too, though a little older. *Don Efraín* always lovingly caressed *Doña Fela's* face when he came home, and gave her a kiss and a hug. And like *Mami*, *Doña Fela* always bathed and changed her clothes and put on fresh lipstick and perfume before he arrived. After *Don Efraín* arrived from work and freshened up, they always sat and talked for at least a half-hour before dinner, while Brenda and I played in her room. Sometimes, *Doña Fela* made him a cocktail, other times they'd have tea or lemonade. This was their re-entry ritual. After about an hour, *Don Efraín* would check in on Brenda and they'd spend some time together before dinner, which was my cue to go home.

Doña Fela and *Don Efraín* were very strict, yet warm and

loving like *Mami* and *Papito*. Since they had only one child to keep track of, it was easier for them to keep a beautiful house and watch over their daughter, but it was harder on Brenda.

My other good friend, Rosemarie, lived on the first floor in Apartment 1, with her eighty-six-year-old grandmother, *Doña Providencia*, who watched over the kids as well as the adults. She was always checking out the front window to see who came in and out, and who was on the stoop. It's as if she were the neighborhood police always keeping an eye out for her brood.

Upstairs, on the fourth floor in Apartment 8, lived *Doña Casilda*, whom we called *Comadre*, and her big family. Our real godmother, *Delis*, lived in Bogota, New Jersey and visited us often, but in Puerto Rican and Hispanic cultures you often adopt people into the family and call them *Comay*, *Compay* or *Madrina and Padrino* and sometimes even *Tia y Tio*. We're really into this extended family concept.

Doña Casilda and her husband, Don Alfredo, had five children. It seemed like all she ever did was cook, clean, feed children and wait on *Don Alfredo* when he was home. The only way she got a break was when *Mami* had me babysit so she could take *Doña Casilda* out shopping, or when we all went to Prospect Park or Orchard Beach together. I helped her out and made money by ironing for *La Comadre*. Once a week I'd go upstairs and she'd give me a pillowcase jammed with clothes that needed ironing, mostly cotton shirts and handkerchiefs for her husband and son, and dresses for her and her girls. I always found it curious that though she had two daughters at home, I was paid to do the ironing for her, but I needed the money so I didn't say anything. I not only ironed for her but also did the ironing in my house, except that there I didn't get paid. I ironed a lot in those days and got to point where I hated the task, and sometimes avoided doing my own clothes. I'd fold and flatten them out neatly and pile books on them or put them under my mattress so they looked pressed.

Next to *La Comadre* in apartment No. 7, lived the only Jewish people in our building: Mr. Eisen, who owned the soda fountain candy store on Longwood Avenue, and his sister, Miss Eisen. I never knew their first names because everyone always addressed them as Mr. Eisen and Miss Eisen. I stopped at Mr. Eisen's soda fountain at least twice a week, once just to visit him and say hello and then again to have my weekly ice cream treat. It was an old-ashioned soda shop with chrome stools that I could swirl around on, covered with marbleized red plastic to match the counter top. I liked Mr. Eisen's company so much I'd often sit reading a book or work on my homework while he took care of his customers.

Mr. Eisen's sundaes and egg creams were the best, and famous from Longwood Avenue all the way to Hunts Point, which was two train stops away. On Sundays, my favorite ritual was to stop by after Mass and buy an ice cream sundae with what was left of my allowance after I made my contribution to the church kitty. "*Hola*," he'd say, "one pistachio Sundae with all the trimmings coming up for *Sinoreeta Aureeta*." He'd take one of the tall heavy fancy glasses, put in two huge scoops of ice cream, ladle lots of rich gooey hot chocolate fudge over that, then pile the sundae high with whipped cream and top it off with a rainbow of sprinkles. I'd sit and eat it as slowly as possible, savoring each rich, creamy bite, and lick the spoon clean after each mouthful.

Once I was done, I'd jump off the stool, slap a quarter on the counter and walk out with a big smile on my face, waving, "*Gracias*, see you back home, Mr. Eisen." Hands on his hips, he'd smile and shake his head saying "How can you have a big ice cream sundae like that every week and be so skinny, Raquelita?" I'd shrug my shoulders and wave goodbye, saying, "I don't know. *Abuelita* says I have a little worm in my stomach that eats it all up, but I hope not."

"Don't forget to say hello to your parents" was always his last phrase. It was his reminder to me that he'd surely mention my being at the shop that day to my parents, so I might as well beat him to it. That's the extended family at work again.

Around the corner on Fox Street was *La Bodega.* When *Mami* or *Abuelita* sent me on an errand to *La Bodega,* I'd practically fly around the corner. If I shopped quickly, I could sneak into the building next door to see my friend *Neli,* and we could hang out on her stoop to ogle all the gorgeous guys. I was so naive. Little did I know at the time that all those cute guys were junkies and up to no good, including *Neli's* brother, who had me walking on cloud nine because he was so tall, dark and handsome. I'd melt inside if he just glanced in my direction, and when he'd say *Hola,* I'd practically faint. But, if *Don Paco,* the bodega owner, caught me hanging out on *Neli's* stoop for too long, he'd surely come out and send me home and, of course, tell *Abuela* or *Mami* or *Papito* when next they stopped by.

Don Paco's bodega was a great place. *Abuela* always said *"tienen de todo un poco":* toothpaste, Campbell's soup, Corn Flakes, Mahtza balls, Palmolive soap, aspirins, and even Kotex sanitary napkins. He also had *platanos, yucca,* rice, beans, avocado and Puerto Rican herbs and spices like *recao* that *Abuela* used in her cooking. And for a penny you could buy these tasty red lollipops from the Island that were shaped like roosters or upside-down flower pots and had a peppery cherry flavor. She was right: *Don Paco* had everything.

Don Paco's bodega was also the local place for information. The men in the neighborhood, including *Papito,* stopped by at least once a day to have *un cafécito* and discuss *las noticias.* Often times I'd find *Papito* and *Don Alfredo, Don Efrain,* and even Mr. Eisen passionately talking about the status of Puerto Rico, President Eisenhower's latest edict, or the latest gang fight and how the neighborhood was going to hell. As they sipped their coffee and debated the latest issues, I often wondered how they understood each other, with all those accents, speaking at the same time.

Don Paco was the only *bodega* owner who would let you buy things on the *fiao* basis, meaning on credit. He kept this big black book with lots of lines and columns. Every client had his or her own page and each time you purchased something he'd put in the date, the item(s) and the amount owed him, and then he asked you sign for it and at the end of each month customers had to clear up the account. Sometimes, if you were reliable, like *Mami* and *Abuela* were, he'd give you a break and let you pay half and carry the other half to the next month. But, after that, you had to clear up the account or pay cash for your purchases until it was paid up. According to *Mami*, he only had trouble with two or three families. Fortunately, no family at 748 Beck Street was on his *delinquente* list. And if *Don Paco* observed us misbehaving or hanging out with the wrong people, believe you me, he'd tell *Mami* or *Papito* the next time they were in the shop. So, if you were someplace you weren't supposed to be, or hanging out with people who weren't from the neighborhood and one of our extended family neighbors or storeowners saw you, they intervened. They scolded you or scared the other kids away, and of course, they always reported the event, no matter how minor, to your parents.

My extended family began in my apartment, then spread throughout the building at 748 Beck Street and went around the corner to Mr. Eisen's Ice Cream Parlor on Longwood Avenue, and to *Don Paco's bodega* on the corner of Fox Street. In fact, this extended family communication system had tentacles as far as our elementary school five blocks away, where either your friends, parents, or worse, the teachers, reported all the comings and goings and happenings. There were eyes watching over us all the time.

5

EL PIANO

One of the great surprises of our move to Beck Street was that our apartment came with a piano. *El Piano,* as Venus and I immediately nicknamed it, was made of heavy dark mahogany wood with beautiful carvings on the front with fancy legs, and its own matching round stool that twirled. Maybe it was always there and got passed down from tenant to tenant, or maybe it was too big and heavy to move. Whatever the reason the previous tenants had for leaving it behind, we lucked out. Up until then Venus and I didn't have any favorite things to do together, but she loved *El Piano* as much as I did and began fiddling with it the day we moved in. It became our connection, our neutral space to share together in joy, our new friend. It united my sister and me, offering a connection to music and to each other as well as a distraction from our usual sibling rivalries. We'd fiddle on it while dinner was being made or while the adults chatted on Sunday afternoons after church while reading the paper. It stood majestically dominating the dining room waiting to be touched and included in our conversations there. It belonged in that room as if it had lived there all its life, almost as if they had built the apartment around it.

I had been a singer since I can remember. I'd spend the better part of any day singing to myself. If I was sad or lonely, afraid or happy, I sang. I sang when I worked and when I played. Sometimes I'd even hum to myself when I was reading. When we lived with *Abuela,* I'd listen to the radio with her and learn the romantic *boleros* of El Trio Los Panchos or the *Serenatas* of Rafael Hernandez, one of Puerto Rico's most prolific composers. One of my favorite songs was the one that *Abuelo* sang to *Abuela* about dreaming that he'd kissed her under the palm tree titled *"Desvelo de Amor,"* a happy dream. *Mami*'s favorite songs for me to sing to her were "Autumn Leaves," "Autumn in New York" and *"Alfonsina y El Mar."* Funny, they all began with the letter "A" and were melancholy songs. Singing was my dream and made me joyful. It's what I wanted to be—a singer!

When I was older, I sang on the Saturday morning radio program called *Star Time* on WNYC. I belonged to the school choirs from elementary through to high school, and was selected as a member of the All City Choir in my junior and senior years. I remember my first leading role as the first soprano of the All City Choir during the Christmas season of 1962 at the opening of Lincoln Center. It was a beautiful, crisp clear winter day, and I saw *Mami* from the veranda of Alice Tully Hall as snowflakes nestled on her hat and shoulders, and tears of joy steamed down her face when I sang the solo in *La Bacarole.* The next year I played Marion, the librarian in *The Music Man,* and the year after that I was in *The Mikado.* I was sure I'd be discovered some day and become famous.

Venus couldn't sing a note, but she took to the keyboard naturally and slowly taught herself to play. I'd sing the songs and she'd find the notes on the piano until she got the tune. She was amazing. This became our daily special ritual—one we shared together during the first few years we lived on Beck Street. When we were with *El Piano,* we didn't fight, we didn't argue, we just had a good time. Whenever there was a special occasion, like a birthday or Christmas or people came to visit, Venus and I would always plan a show.

That's how I came up with the idea for our sister act *Las Chicas.* I figured if we worked hard enough, we'd become really good, then we'd become famous and make lots of money so we could buy a beautiful house to move the family from El Bronx to the suburbs of Long Island or Connecticut.

One day shortly after my tenth birthday, Venus and I overheard *Mami* and *Papito* talking about what to do now that he'd lost his maintenance job. *Papito* had a dream too, which was to be his own boss and open a second-hand furniture store.

> *"Mira Pedrito,"* Mami said, "maybe this is a blessing. You can't work all day and start a business, so why not start now that you have free time."
>
> "Pero, mi amor, are you sure?"
>
> "Si, *Papito,* I'm sure, it'll be difficult, but we'll make it work."

Their plan was to use their savings, raise the rent contribution from Sylvia, and to our utter disbelief, sell *El Piano.* "They can't sell *El Piano,* they just can't," Venus and I uttered simultaneously. Devastated and angered by what I'd just overheard, we tiptoed back to our bedroom and I immediately started working on a plan to raise money and keep the family from selling *El Piano.* For once, Venus was my trusted ally.

First I decided to ask the neighbors for work, beginning with *La Comadre,* who always needed babysitting and help with the ironing and household chores. Despite the fact that I already had plenty of housework to do in my own apartment and I hated ironing, we couldn't lose *El Piano,* we just couldn't, so I forged ahead. I asked *Doña Provi* and even asked Miss Eisen who, like my mother, hated housework. They agreed. I'd work one day per week for each of them after school for two hours, which meant I couldn't go to the Police Athletic League (PAL) after school, which I'd just begun doing as a member of the track team. But it was worth it, because I'd make an extra six dollars a week to contribute to the household expenses—that's twenty-four dollars per month.

Venus, who was as lazy as they come, found the perfect not-too-strenuous way to make extra money. She decided to make and sell fresh lemonade and Kool-Aid on our front stoop daily throughout the summer. We didn't know how much money Venus would make selling refreshments, but this time she agreed to help me with my household chores by keeping our room clean, which for her was a big deal. By the end of the week we had our plan in place and decided to tell *Mami* and *Papito* that Friday night at dinnertime.

Friday afternoon as we walked home from school, we saw a big truck in front of our building. I felt my throat tightening as I began running up the block. As I got closer, I saw these two big burly men with wide leather belts around their waists carrying *El Piano* out of our building. *Abuelo* was giving directions in Spanish as the moving guy, with *El Piano* strapped on his back, looked at him like he was crazy.

"Man, this damn thing is too damn heavy, I gotta put it down."

"Yes," I screamed. "Put it down, you can't do that." I started yelling at *Papito*, "What are you doing, *no puedes*, you can't sell it. I've got more work ironing and cleaning, I'll be making extra money, twenty-four dollars a month, and Venus is going to work too, you can have it all but please, please, *Papito*, don't sell *El Piano*," I pleaded.

Mami yelled down from the window.

"Raquel, Venus, get away from there. Can't you see these men are working? You'll cause an accident."

"But, *Mami*," I pleaded as I looked at Venus who was stunned and silent. "Please, don't sell *El Piano*," I begged hysterically, "Venus will do my chores at home so I can work to make money. I'm gonna iron for *La Comadre* and Ms. Eisen. I'll give you all the money I make," I pleaded, tears gushing.

"Both of you, come upstairs at once," she demanded.

I raced up the stairs crying, and *Mami*, *Abuela* and *Titi María* greeted me at the door. Venus stayed downstairs silent, not shedding a tear, staring at the piano movers.

"Didn't I tell you she'd be upset?" *Titi Maria* mumbled under her breath to *Mami*.

"Aha," followed *Abuela*, *"te lo dije,* I told you."

"Raquel, sit down, stop crying and listen. We need the money and that's that. We sold it for six hundred dollars, do you realize that's six months' rent and food. It would take you two years to make that kind of money and we need it now so *Papito* can start his business. But there's good news. It'll still be in the family, sort of."

"In the family? Did you sell it to Cousin Gladys' family in Brooklyn?"

"No," my mother replied, still trying to placate me.

"To *Madrina Delis* in New Jersey?" I pressed.

"No."

"Well then, who, we don't know or visit anybody else."

"We sold it to the PAL, right across the street, *Mijita*, so you and Venus can still use it."

"But *Mami*, the Police Athletic League is a public center for kids, everyone will use it; they'll get their fingerprints on it or write graffiti all over it, they'll destroy it. Besides, *El Piano* is like a member of our family, we can't sell a member of the family."

"El Piano is an object, young lady," *Mami* said firmly, "and we need the money. Now that's that!"

"Well, that's not it for me. I don't care, I'll never forgive you and *Papito* for selling it."

I went to my room, locked myself in and cried myself to

sleep. Later that night *Mami* came into my room, trying to be nice to me.

"*Mijita,* please, we have to talk."

"You mean you have to talk, you don't care what I have to say!"

"Young lady, you don't speak to me that way."

"Why, are you gonna punish me or hit me? Go ahead, I don't care. To you it was just piece of furniture, but to me it was my dream, my plan for *Las Chicas* and for the family. Now it's gone. I don't care. I'm never going to the PAL again!"

"Well, *Mija, perdoname,* but we did what we had to do for the family."

"I won't forgive you," I whimpered back.

I was really pushing my luck. I'm surprised she didn't slap me.

The next day, after breakfast, I visited *La Comadre,* Ms. Eisen and *Doña Provi,* and told them I changed my mind and wouldn't be working for them. "Why should I do all that extra housework, which I hate, if it's not going to help me keep *El Piano!*" I told them.

Then, even though I never went to the center on the weekends, I went to the PAL and sat and stared at the piano. They had put a lock on it. I stroked and caressed it like you would a pet or a friend who was moving far away, and cried my heart out. Now you had to get special permission from the Director's Office to get the key to use it. The problem was I couldn't play and Venus was too young to go to the PAL. For weeks, I'd go to the center and sit on the piano stool, staring at it and crying; I'd talk to it and caress it like I did my cracked-up doll, *Doña Missy.* And, true to my word, I gave my parents the silent treatment at breakfast and dinner for over a month. I only answered direct questions and after dinner just went to my room, sat rocking on my bed in the dark, and cried.

About two months later, they put a notice on the PAL bulletin board that a piano teacher would be giving lessons for two dollars a session to members. I guess that was better than nothing, but we'd have to wait two more years until Venus was eight before she could join the PAL, which she never did. Venus never mentioned *El Piano* again. It's as if *El Piano* had died and she locked up her feelings about it in some dark place in her heart like she always did when things hurt her. Eventually I stopped sitting by *El Piano* and stroking it and I gave up the idea of the *Las Chicas* singing duo.

Three months after *El Piano* was sold, *Papito* opened his own business. It was a second-hand furniture store and moving company called *Casa Castaño* on Jackson Avenue by the elevated train station. I have a worn sepia-tone photo of *Papito* proudly standing in front of his store in his working clothes and cap with a big smile on his face. Though I was happy for *Papito*, to me the dining room always felt a little empty like its heart had been taken out. Months later, *Papito* found and restored an antique piece of furniture called a breakfront that was placed where *El Piano* used to live. Venus and I looked at it in disgust, and without ever discussing it, neither of us would ever lean on it or place anything on top of the breakfront, nor ever search for anything inside of it. *El Piano* was gone and our one special connection severed. To this day, some forty years later, we have not recaptured that indelible jubilant connection that *El Piano* offered us.

6

AUTUMN LEAVES

On this beautiful crisp clear autumn day, the leaves crackling underneath my shoes, I hummed *Autumn Leaves* as I walked home hand in hand with my new friend Lillie. When we reached her stoop I continued singing and waved so long heading homeward. "See you tomorrow morning, Lillie, OK!"

Lillie was from Elizabeth City, North Carolina and came to our fourth-grade class in the middle of the fall semester. She was pretty, with very high cheekbones, like *Titi María*. Her eyes were sad, but her smile was friendly and so big it took up her entire face. They sat Lillie next to me in the back of the classroom on her first day of school and I liked her right away. She liked me instantly too, and during recess we agreed to walk home together. On our first walk we discovered we had many things in common, we loved to read, liked jumping rope and playing jacks. And, best of all, she was a singer too! Our styles were different though, I was into blues and romantic singing and Lillie sang religious gospel church songs. Sometimes we'd walk home holding hands and sing out loud ignoring the stares from passersby.

When I reached the corner of Fox and Kelly, something made me turn back. I saw that Lillie was still on her stoop hunched over her books tightly. There was a group of older boys in front of her stoop leaning against a car, talking loud and teasing her. Lillie looked nervous and scared so I turned around and walked back toward her.

Turning back was risky, because it meant I'd get home late and *Mami* expected me to be home by a 3:15 or 3:20 the absolute latest. Twenty minutes was the amount of time *Mami* calculated it should take me to get home. So, if I didn't arrive within that amount of time, she'd be on the lookout for me, worried or angry or more likely, both.

The fact was I usually couldn't wait much longer than 3:20 to get home anyway, because by that time my bladder was almost always bursting to let go of the milk and juice we'd had during snack time and lunch. My teachers at PS 62 rarely let us go to the bathroom, except during recess or lunch when the lines were long and the bell would ring before you could make it. So *Mami* and I had a special routine for when I arrived. By 3:15 she'd be looking out of the front window expecting to see me turn the corner, then she'd buzz me in and quickly open the apartment door wide open. When I could, I'd race up the stairs, which is really difficult when you're holding your legs tight to keep from peeing on yourself, throw my books on the floor and head straight for the bathroom. Sometimes the warm pee would dribble down my legs as I climbed the stairs, which was embarrassing and made me angry. Other times, I could barely make it up the stairs, and I'd have to stop every couple of steps to squeeze my legs together, slowly crawling all the way up to the apartment then down our long hallway to the bathroom like a semi-crippled person. That's when my stomach really hurt. When this happened I'd get goose bumps all over my skin after I peed. I never understood why with so many bathrooms in school they didn't let us use them, but teachers had a lot of strange rules back then. Now I was worried about Lillie because she looked so scared, so I forgot I had to go to the bathroom. Maybe I just didn't have that burning urge to pee because I didn't drink the tomato juice they gave us during recess. I hated V-8, it tasted grainy like it had sand in it and it wasn't sweet. Juice is supposed to be sweet, isn't it?

"Is anything wrong," I asked?
Lillie looked up with tears in her eyes and said,
"Yeah my mother isn't home yet. I have to sit here and wait for her and those guys scare me."
Beck Street is a pretty dangerous neighborhood, which is why *Mami* was so strict about what time I got home from school and about my always playing right in front of our building. Lillie lived on Fox Street, which was an even more dangerous neighborhood because it's where many of the gangs hung out. At about three in the afternoon they all seemed to come out of the woodwork and take over the street corners, stoops and hallways, talking, crooning and showing off their insignia jackets. It must be where the term "shucking and jiving" came from because that's all they did, strut around and comb back their slicked down hair. Each gang had the same style shiny satin jacket with brightly embroidered letters in their own colors: The Sinners, The Crowns and The Dragons were from our neighborhood, Fox Street. The only girl gang, The Turbanettes, wore Turquoise jackets and turbans. I thought they looked ridiculous.
"Don't stay here alone, Lillie, come home with me."
I ripped out a blank page from my black and white marbled covered notebook and wrote a note telling Lillie's mother that she was scared and that I took her home with me. I wrote down our phone number and *Mami*'s name on it, Dina, short for *Enedina*. I stuck it in the mailbox then we walked hand in hand toward my place as the guys jeered at us.

"What's the matter, girlie, you scared or something? Gotta have a chaperone, huh?" they booed as we passed by them. They followed us for a while jeering loudly, "Hey skinny minnie, hey little black girl."

I pulled Lillie along and we started running. When we turned the corner to my apartment building I immediately heard *Mami*'s angry voice and the buzzer.

"You're late! Where have you been, young lady?"

As I reached the door, I suddenly had to pee desperately, so I dropped my books and said "*Mami*, this is my classmate from school, Lillie."

I raced down the hallway. It was another close call. Gosh I hated that hall, it was too damn long.

When I returned, I found *Mami* and Lillie standing right where I left them, staring at each other. *Mami* had this "I'm not very pleased" expression on her face as she asked,

"*¿Y esta muchacha?*

"I told you, *Mami*, this is Lillie, she's in my home room at school, we sit right next to each other." She was sitting alone on her stoop because her mother is working late and there were lots of gang boys around, so I told her to come home with me. We left a note for her mom, Mrs. Banks, to call you," I said, frowning at her.

She spoke in Spanish in front of Lillie, which she'd always said was rude. She made another face then pointed toward the dining room and gave us milk and cookies.

"*Vayan afuera*—go outside and play when you're done," she instructed sternly, and with a wave of her hand, dismissed us."

Again, I was puzzled, she didn't even ask about my homework. What is wrong with her today, I wondered?

After about an hour, *Mami* called us upstairs and said we had to do our homework. But this time she said we should do it in my room, instead of at the dining room table where she could watch as she worked in the kitchen. She asked us what we had to do.

"Our favorite *Mami,* I have a composition to do."
"*Pues,* do it" she said curtly, and walked off.

Mami was acting so weird. She was usually very friendly when meeting new people, especially kids, and she loved doing homework with me, compositions were her favorite, but this time she left us alone. So off we walked to my bedroom. Lillie sat at one end of my bed and I on the other. Luckily, Venus was playing with her friend upstairs, so we had the room to ourselves. When we finished our homework it was dinnertime.

Lillie's mother hadn't called yet, so I invited her to eat with us. Again, *Mami* looked at me with this face like I was about to get a spanking, but I just ignored her and began setting the table.

Abuela and *Abuelo* came in from their nap and sat down. Then Sylvia, our tenant, arrived and also scrunched up her eyebrows just like *Mami.* She pursed her lips and jutted them out in the typical Puerto Rican gesture that looks like a kiss, but isn't. Without a word being spoken, that jutting facial expression could mean a thousand things "*¿Y esa*" (who's that?), "Who dragged this one in" or "Did you see what she's wearing?" or "I don't like the looks of her." Almost always, it was judgmental, disapproving or mocking, and I hoped and prayed Lillie didn't notice.

Soon Venus ran in. Thank goodness the first words out of her mouth were,

"Yuck, I smell spinach, I hate vegetables especially green ones."

When she noticed Lillie she began talking to her in a friendly way as if she'd always known her.

"Hi Lillie, what's up, you don't like spinach either huh? Don't blame you."

For once she did something right. Throughout the entire meal the adults all spoke in Spanish, asking questions about Lillie: "Who is this *Nena Extraña*" and *Mami,* the bilingual adult kept replying in Spanish *"mas tarde,"* I'll explain later. Each time *Mami* said this Lillie looked down at her lap and closed her eyes tight.

"Let's eat fast, Venus, you too, Lillie, so we can go to our room and play."

Just as I was about to ask for dessert, the doorbell rang. It was Lillie's mother, Mrs. Banks. It was about 7:30. She caressed my face and thanked me for bringing Lillie home, and gave *Mami* a jar of jam. Again, *Mami* was curt, barely opening her mouth to say "Thank you" and she didn't even shake Mrs. Banks' extended hand, after taking the jar of jam. Whatever is wrong with her, I wondered.

When Mrs. Banks and Lillie left I cornered *Mami* in the foyer.

"What is wrong with you today?"

"Nada Mija, what do you mean?"

"Well, you've been acting kind of weird, *Mami,* what's wrong?" After what seemed like ten minutes she replied,

"Well I was just a little shocked that you would bring that girl home".

"She's not *that girl,* her name is Lillie. She's my girlfriend from school; sits next to me in class and we walk halfway home from school together every day. Besides, I told you it was dangerous on her stoop, *Mami.* "I don't understand, why don't you like Lillie;" "she's good and respectful." *"Mija,* I was just distracted."

"So distracted that you couldn't even shake her mother's hand? That's rude, isn't it?"

"Don't be fresh, young lady," hands immediately on her hips, signaling danger.

"Well something is wrong. You kept looking at Lillie like she was from Mars or something, and all of you grown-ups kept making faces at the dinner table. Don't deny it, I saw all of you do it many times. You made her feel bad, didn't you see her crying?"

"Ay mija," she sighed, "its just that you shouldn't bring anybody home like that."

"Like that? Like what?" *"Pues mija,* she's a *negrita,* she's black, you know. "Huh?" I was stunned. Suddenly *Mami* looked very small to me. I backed away from her then walked off without asking permission, fighting the tears of anger and confusion I felt welling up. Sometimes Mami and I were in synch, like about school and singing and my plans, but other times like now, she confused me.

I thought to myself, *Abuelo* told me that Puerto Ricans are mixed, we're from Spain and Africa, and we have Indian blood too, from the Taino Arawak tribe, which is why his skin is a rich reddish brown color. He said he's *mestizo,* so what's the big deal. I couldn't believe what I'd just heard come from *Mami's* lips. I turned around and yelled, "Well, *negrita* or not, she's my friend and I like her, period!"

I locked myself in my room and sat crying in the dark.

Mami and I hardly spoke the next morning before I left for school, and that evening at the dinner table as the red beans and *arroz con pollo* were being passed around, *Abuelo* asked, *"¿Y esa mucha extraña?* Who was that strange looking girl?"

"Si" Sylvia chimed in almost in unison with grandpa. "What was she doing here, where did she come from?"

Now I was puzzled, these questions were coming from *Abuelo.*

I jumped up from my chair, stomped my foot on the ground and yelled.

"There is nothing strange about Lillie, what are you talking about?"

"Hay Raquel", Sylvia said, *"es que* you don't *bring "los morenitos"* home."

Again, with this. It's like a disease and it's spreading, handed down from generation to generation. There is a myth that Puerto Ricans are not prejudiced, but I painfully found out, and in my own home with my family, that we are. Sylvia continued her litany.

"*Hay que mejorar la raza*. We must improve the race, *mija*. You can play with them, but you don't bring them home and you don't marry them."

"I have no intention of marrying Lillie." I yelled, and stormed off hiding my angry tears. My family is prejudiced, plain and simple. How did they get this way? What's even stranger is that *Abuelo* has very dark brown skin and a wide nose like Lillie's mother, and *Mami* has *pelo crespo*, kinky hair, she says all the time. How could they be that way? It's wrong. I'll show them.

That weekend, I decided to speak to *Papito* about it while I helped him with his special project, the homemade stereo speakers he was building from scratch. I usually helped by handing him tools as he worked or read and translated the instructions. Mostly though I just kept him company and we talked. I told *Papito* about Lillie's visit and how everybody was rude and acted so strange. *Papito* worked at night so he was rarely home for dinner during the week. Not wanting to take sides against *Mami*, *Papito* said, "*es una pena,*" it's a pity that people are always looking for someone to feel superior to and look down upon and that just because the world works that way doesn't make it right. "*Quizas*, perhaps some day people will change," he said, looking out into space, "*quizas*." Like the song, "Perhaps, Perhaps, Perhaps," he kept repeating the word. Then he suddenly yelled "*coño!*" He'd hammered his finger instead of the nail. He walked away, I thought, to put on a band-aide, but when he returned, he had two books in hands. One had a cartoon on the cover and was about Jose Marti, a black leader from Cuba who wanted independence for the slaves.

"Oh, I know him *Papito*, they have a statue of Don Martí on a horse in Central Park."

"*Si querida*, it's a beautiful statue.

The other book was about *Pedro Albízu Campos*, a *mulatto* Puerto Rican nationalist who also believes in independence for his country."

That night, I asked Venus,

"Did you see the way they treated my friend Lillie at dinner?" Venus, who was preoccupied with selecting what to wear to school the next day, responded,

"Ay Raquel, you worry too much about things you can't do anything about. Just stay away from that Lillie, that's all."

"Not you too!"

I turned out the lights and began to think out a plan.

On the stoop the next day, I confided in my other friend Rosemarie, who retorted,

"You're lucky your mother just made faces. My *Abuela*, *Doña Provi*, would probably kill me if I ever brought a black person home."

God, I thought, is everybody like this?

The following Saturday evening I surprised *Mami* with a dinner guest. She looked stunned as she turned around to place the oblong plate of *picadillo* on the table and saw Lillie on my left. Hand on hip still holding the oblong plate of tasty ground meat in mid air, her facial expression went from shocked to angry to quizzical. She shrugged her shoulders and began to laugh as a big smile spread across her face.

"Oh well, in a Puerto Rican house there's always room for one more at the table. You are bold, young lady, I'll give you that."

I introduced Lillie to *Papito* who was seated on her left, and to *Titi María*. *Papito* was very nice to Lillie, as he shook her hand saying, "*Hola, bienvenida*, welcome!" I brought Lillie home once a week every month, for the rest of the school year, which drove Sylvia nuts because she had to behave. I loved watching her squirm.

At the end of the school year I was excited when Ms. MacCauly asked me to read my latest composition to the class. As I passed by Lillie, I whispered in her ear, "This is for you Lillie, my dear friend."

Color, what is color anyway? When you're a kid color is just a word that describes the crayons we use in art class or the clothes we wear. It's not till you're older that you're taught it's something more. This week I learned that the color of people's skin is sometimes a problem and I'm sad to say, I learned this in my own home from my own family. This week I learned that my family is prejudiced.

I'll never forget the look of surprise on my mother's face, when I brought a new girlfriend home. At the time I couldn't figure out what it meant, but I soon found out. I never really thought about the color of her skin, though I saw she was dark. My new friend was my age and friendly. She liked playing jacks and jumping rope like me. I brought her home one day because she was lonely and scared waiting on the stoop for her mother to get home from work. I didn't pay much attention to the color of her skin until it became a problem for Mami, and the rest of the family. I was shocked and angry when I heard what Mami and the other adults said.

They said, "You can play with them—them meaning "los negritos"—but don't bring them home. And, you don't marry them either, we need to better the race, you see."

Well, these are lessons I refused to learn.

During autumn, people are always saying how beautiful the leaves look when they change colors. Maybe people should change colors too. The whites should become black or brown or "mulatta" like me, and the blacks should become white for a while. Then they'd each see how it hurts to be rejected because of your skin color or because you're different. Perhaps then they'd learn to see that your outside is a part of you, a gift from God that no one should make judgements about or make fun of. Maybe then they'd learn that when you hurt people because of how they look on the outside, you hurt them

on the inside, in their hearts and mind and souls, the place
where we're all the same.

When I finished I looked up and saw a stunned look on Mrs. MacCauley's face, but Lillie's eyes gleamed with pride. As went back to my seat she hugged me. Though I lost touch with her after that school year, as her family returned to North Carolina, Lillie has always remained in my heart—for it was through her I learned one of the most important lessons of my life.

7

SMOKE GETS IN MY EYES

My friend, Rosemarie, was a skinny, six-foot-tall girl, and like me, she wore glasses. She was very smart, a bit of a spoiled brat, and lived with her grandmother, *Doña Provi* (short for Providencia) in Apartment 1 on the first floor of our building.

Doña Provi was old-fashioned, very strict and very clean. She wore her silver white hair braided and wrapped in a huge bun either at the top of her head to make her taller, or at the nape of her neck like Flamenco dancers. She changed her housedress every day and wore old-fashioned black nun's shoes—the ones with thick short heels that tied up with laces. All her shirtwaist cotton dresses were the same A-line shape, with buttons up the front and a matching belt. She sewed them herself, only the color changed: yellow on Monday, light blue on Tuesday, pink on Wednesday, pale green on Thursday and white on Friday. Saturday was the heavy-duty cleaning day when we did the hallway as well, so she repeated one of the colors from the week. On Sunday she wore her navy blue crepe dress-suit or her black suit, with black shoes and a white hat with a veil and gloves. She always wore white gloves.

Even though Rosemarie towered over *Doña Provi*, her grandmother was the one person she was totally scared of, though it didn't stop her from getting into mischief. *Doña Provi* walked around with her special weapon practically tied to her hip. This weapon had a very misleading name, *la chancleta,* which meant "slipper," but there was nothing delicate about *la chancleta*. It was a simple object made of three parts. The most important part was an old leather shoe sole that was nailed onto part two, a hard wooden stick, and the last part was a rope perfectly sized to fit around her wrist. I used to think *Doña Provi* carried her *chancleta* everywhere, hanging from her wrist or her belt, but in fact she kept many *chancletas* hanging by the doors in various rooms of her apartment. There was one in the kitchen, one in the bedroom, another in the living room and one in the dining room. She even had one hanging in her foyer by the front door entrance so she could shake it at us and chase us up the stairs threateningly if we were found loitering in the hallway. She'd open her door yelling, "*Que hacen?* What are you doing in the hallway, don't you have a home?" as the *chancleta* vibrated in her strong wrinkled hand. Slippers are usually soft and warm and fuzzy, but believe me this slipper was hard and made a snappy sound.

Doña Provi's favorite pastime was sitting by the window of her first-floor apartment, watching *los kids,* as she called them, coming and going. As the oldest adult in our building, even older than my grandparents, *Doña Provi* believed it was her job to keep us kids out of mischief, sort of like our own private truant officer at 748 Beck Street. She must have been at least fifty years old when she was born, and though now she was in her eighties and you'd expect her not to be able to chase us around, she had the energy of a twenty-five-year old where her self-proclaimed, truant-officer duties were concerned.

Many times throughout the day we'd hear the sharp crackle of her weapon snapping against a wall, the kitchen table or on the sofa, scaring the daylights out of one child or another. Sometimes she'd snap it against her thighs, *"Quieres? You want this?"* she'd taunt, pointing *la chancleta* at you menacingly. "It's right here waiting for you," she'd say, with a very terse look on her face. *Doña Provi* and her special homemade weapon were famous for blocks and blocks, so much so that the few kids from other neighborhoods who played on our block were always on their best behavior and ever so courteous in her presence. I'll bet their parents would have liked to see that.

I remember seeing *Doña Provi* hit Rosemarie with *la chancleta* only once when she whacked her hard on her calves for saying *coño,* a curse word. Though her bark was louder than her bite, the threat of *la chancleta*'s use was ever present.

Puerto Ricans are known for speaking expressively using our hands, arms and bodies, as if we were conducting an orchestra. It looks and sounds like we're yelling, when in fact, we're just speaking passionately. In spring and summer, when our windows and doors are open, you hear everything in the neighborhood, especially in the interior courtyard, where the sounds bounce off the brick walls. Mothers summoning their kids home for lunch or dinner, dogs barking, children laughing gleefully, and of course, sirens howling. In this mix, *Doña Provi*'s *chancleta*-snapping was a perfect fit and came through loud and crisply.

If she wasn't sitting by her window protecting us, she was always busy around the house cleaning, sewing, moving furniture, changing curtains or cooking. She and *Abuela* were the best cooks in the building and always made something scrumptious to eat. And, in complete contradiction to her heavy-handed scolding and *chancletta*-snapping tactics, was her baking of delicious pastries for the kids in the building. Her other occupation was to watch over Rosemarie like a hawk—hardly ever letting her out of her sight. I was the only girlfriend she was allowed to play with or visit their apartment.

We were twelve years old when Rosemarie cajoled me into following her down to our basement, saying she had a secret to share with me. When your father is the super in your building, you have access to the boiler room, which is a good place to hide and yet be able to hear when you're being summoned. Rosemarie, Brenda and I spent many hours hiding in the basement, sharing stories, secrets and dreams. As I followed Rosemarie, I kept asking, "Will you tell me the secret already, what is it?" The secret, as it turned out, was in a small, brown, carved wooden box that Rosemarie pulled from a space on the wall in the boiler room where a brick was missing. She opened it to reveal a pack of Lucky Strike cigarettes, the one with the big red circle in the middle and the slogan "Lucky Strike means fine tobacco" underneath.

"I've decided I want company, Raquel, so it's time for you to learn to smoke," Rosemarie declared as she struck a match, lit the cigarette, then blew out the smoke dramatically like an actress with years of smoking experience. She repeated this action many times insisting I watch closely as she showed me how to hold the cigarette and inhale smoke like Bette Davis or Joan Crawford. After a few drags, she passed it on to me. At first I dragged lightly into my mouth, but didn't swallow it, then blew the smoke out, trying to make circles, but got it in my eyes instead. "Ughh, it tastes bitter and burns my tongue," I said to her. "It'll grow on you," she responded like a gym coach, "keep practicing."

After a few puffs, I inhaled deeply, then started hacking and coughing uncontrollably. "Shush, they'll hear you." I started to put out the cigarette, but she whispered, "What, are you crazy? Don't waste it, they cost a fortune." She grabbed the butt from me and finished it off, while I fought the dizziness I felt in my head and the nausea in my stomach.

"OK, I'm done," said Rosemarie, dumping the butt in the boiler, "let's brush our teeth."

"Brush our teeth, with what?"

"Our fingers and some toothpaste I keep hidden here, see?"

Rosemarie was always prepared, especially for mischief. She even had a bottle of Coca-Cola so we could rinse our mouths, and perfume, too. We brushed, gulped a swig of soda, then sprayed ourselves with *Agua de Florida* toilet water and went outside to jump rope.

"Come on, hurry, work up a sweat so that they can't tell we've been smoking."

After about four or five lessons that week, I got better at smoking and we began doing a cigarette almost every day.

"If my voice coach finds out, she would drop me like a hot potato, and get me in a lot of trouble with *Mami*," I said once. But Rosemarie just shrugged it off. "It won't hurt your voice, you silly goose." Fortunately, my voice coach, Ms. Ava, hadn't suspected yet.

Rosemarie's mother, Ginny, visited her every week. She insisted we call her Titi Ginny, because she was too young to be called *Doña* even though she was an adult. Titi Ginny was divorced and remarried, like *Mami*, and now lived on Long Island with her new husband and two new kids. When she divorced, she lived with her daughter at *Doña Provi's* house, until she went off in search of a career. Rosemarie had lived with her grandmother since she was a baby. That's another thing we had in common. *Doña Provi* put her foot down and said she'd keep Rosemarie until Titi Ginny grew up. Instead of a career, Titi Ginny found a second husband. Neither Rosemarie nor *Doña Provi* liked her mother's new husband or his two sons, so she stayed living with her grandmother. Titi Ginny and *Mami* had become good friends and many times the four of us would do things together, like shopping or visiting museums, one of their favorite excursions. I liked them too, even though we had to be very quiet and tiptoe around, something I never understood since everything in the museum was either dead or made of stone. It was another one of those adult rules I couldn't figure out.

The thing about Titi Ginny's visits is that they were always short and usually a surprise so Rosemarie and *Doña Provi* rarely knew when to expect her. Well on this day, as I was finally blowing nice round circles with my cigarette smoke and not getting dizzy or nauseous anymore, Titi Ginny showed up for one of her surprise visits.

Rosemarie was so impressed with my smoking skills, she decided we should do two cigarettes instead of one, so we spent a longer time than usual in the boiler room. Totally into our smoking experience and unaware of anything around us, *Papito*'s assistant, Mr. Gerald, a quiet older black man who tiptoed around the building doing his chores, had decided to check on the boiler. Unbeknownst to us, he saw us smoking and immediately tiptoed up to tell *Doña Provi*, but it was Titi Ginny who opened the door. Suddenly, we heard Titi Ginny's loud sharp voice calling, "Rosemarie, Rosemarie, I know you're down there, come up here at once." Quickly, Rosemarie tried to put out the cigarette, but Titi Ginny ran into the boiler room and caught us red-handed. Rosemarie was blowing smoke out of her mouth and I had the pack in my hands. Titi Ginny slapped the cigarette out of Rosemarie's mouth and simultaneously snatched the Lucky Strike package out of my hand. "Upstairs immediately, both of you!" She sent Rosemarie to her room and then took me up to my apartment.

The minute *Mami* opened the door, Titi Ginny began yelling, "I caught them red-handed, I caught her with the cigarette pack in her hand. Smell her." She yelled, pushing me toward *Mami*, "she was teaching my Rosemarie how to smoke." And of course, *Mami* smelled me, opened her eyes wide and thanked Titi Ginny as she closed the door. *Mami* turned around, raised her right eyebrow, which always spelled trouble, and pointed menacingly toward my room. I began slowly walking down the hallway as *Mami* followed, trembling and thinking to myself, "Oh boy, I'm in for it now!"

It's a funny thing about me, whenever I got caught doing something wrong, there was just nothing I could say in my defense. Everything showed in my eyes: joy, sorrow, guilt, so, head bowed, eyes unable to hide the truth, I walked toward my room praying that the punishment wouldn't be too harsh and secretly promising myself "I must not cry, I will not cry." As we passed the bathroom, *Mami* opened the linen closet door searching for something. I seized the moment and ran to my room, thinking I'd lock the door, then decided against it, knowing that would only make her angrier and get me double jeopardy. I sat on my hands on the edge of the bed waiting for my punishment. *Mami* walked in and to my amazement she pulled out a *chancleta* from behind her back. When did she get that? Unlike *Doña Provi*, who always threatened Rosemarie but rarely used it, *Mami* never threatened. She just spanked my fanny until I couldn't sit. I couldn't control my crying either; I sobbed, no, I wailed uncontrollably. That night and for the next two days I ate standing up at the table and slept on my tummy. It's a good thing it was the weekend otherwise I'd have to stand up in my classroom all day as well. That would really be embarrassing.

The most infuriating thing was that Rosemarie got away with it. Titi Ginny not only didn't tell *Doña Provi*, though she told my mother, she said that I was the one teaching Rosemarie, I was the instigator. Rosemarie didn't get spanked and she didn't even get punished. I was really pissed. After all, I had gotten hit and punished for doing something that she taught me to do so she could have company. I was furious with Titi Ginny for twisting the story. Adults are always demanding you tell the truth, yet they run around keeping secrets, or worse, getting the stories twisted. It wasn't fair.

A few days after the pain began to subside, I sat in my room in the dark listening to music on the phonograph as I planned how to get back at Rosemarie. I did my best thinking sitting and rocking on my bed in the dark while listening to my favorite albums. I kept asking myself, "How will I get back at her?"

I decided I'd use my allowance to buy another pack of cigarettes and put them in the basement. You could do that in those days by just saying they were for your parents. Then I convinced Rosemarie that it was safe to smoke again. After we had each taken a few puffs, I said, "Oh, my God, I've got to run, I forgot I have to go to *la bodega,* see you later." I gave her my unfinished cigarette. Now she had one in each hand. I quickly ran upstairs and made a lot of noise so *Doña Provi* would open the door and ask about Rosemarie, and she did. "She's in the basement," I said. Then I ran around the corner as if I was going to the market, but I sneaked into our courtyard instead. *Doña Provi* got her *chancleta* and a few moments later I heard her exclaim, "Muchacha, what are ju doin'?" she said in her thick accent, *"Que haces?"* She caught Rosemarie in the act and whacked her, once, then twice. That was the second time I actually saw Rosemarie get *la chancleta,* and even then it was only two whacks, yet she wailed like she'd been beaten to within an inch of her life. I couldn't believe what a spoiled ninny she was.

Later that afternoon, though, like the well-trained little Catholic girl I was, the guilt began to well up in me. I asked *Mami* permission to go downstairs, then meekly knocked on *Doña Provi's* door and asked if I could visit with Rosemarie. *Doña Provi* said yes, but only for a short while because she was being punished. I guess Rosemarie didn't realize that I had ratted on her to *Doña Provi.* If she'd seen my face she would have known right away, but she was reading and whimpering, and sort of ignored me when I came in.

I sat next to Rosemarie, put my arm around her and confessed the whole story. I told her how Titi Ginny twisted up the story when she told my mother about the smoking and that it made me really mad, so I decided to get even. I was surprised when she said, "It's OK" and hugged me.

"I also hate it when *Mami* Ginny just shows up and doesn't mind her own business. She breezes in, gets me in trouble and then leaves, like a summer storm. She does that always," she whimpered as tears welled up in her eyes.

Then as we looked at each other we both said simultaneously,

> "You know smoking stinks! "It smells up your clothes and your hair!"
> "Yeah," I chimed in, "and it's really bad for my singing voice." "Let's quit!" Rosemarie said, stomping her foot emphatically.

We shook hands and asked for permission to play on the stoop. *Doña Provi* reluctantly agreed. We ran to the basement, threw the cigarettes into the boiler and watched the package of Lucky Strikes smolder into ashes. Our arms wrapped around each other, we went up to the stoop and began playing jacks two seconds before *Doña Provi* approached the window to check up on us, *chancleta* in hand. Whew!

8

THE TOOTH FAIRY

While seated in the dentist's reception area waiting for my yearly dental check up and cleaning, I overheard Dr. Green saying he wanted the Spanish-speaking people in the neighborhood as clients. "I know they need service and their kids have the worst teeth in school and I could make some extra money too. But, I don't speak the language." Then, he kicked the pump underneath the chair that made the drill begin buzzing.

It was true. There were more Latinos moving into the neighborhood, Puerto Ricans, Cubans and Dominicans were moving to the US looking for work and a better education for their kids. *Papito*'s friends, Carmelina and Paito, had arrived a few weeks ago and slept in the room I shared with my sister while we slept in the living room. Though we all liked having them around, I was glad for them as well as myself when Marta and Mike moved out and they took over that room as tenants. I'd miss the Petrakises, especially Marta, but after four months of opening and closing the sofa bed every night and morning, I was beginning to feel like a tenant in my own home.

I began thinking about Dr. Green's comment and an idea occurred to me. I jumped out of my seat, ran into his workroom and interrupted him. "Dr. Green, Dr. Green," I blurted out, "I can help you, I speak Spanish and English and I need a job. I can talk to the families in the neighborhood and tell them about you and what a good dentist you are. I can work in the reception area and call the clients, make appointments, then greet them and sit them in the chair and put the bib on them and everything. They all work late, so it would have to be in the evenings and on Saturdays. And maybe you could train me as a dental assistant, that way I can earn money now for my singing lessons and when I finish learning and become a good assistant I can earn even more money for college. So what do you think, Mr. Green, isn't that a really great idea? Oh I'm so excited, please say yes, Mr. Green, please, *por favor?* "

"Whoa, slow down," he said, looking at me and wrinkling both his eyebrows. "Slow down a little. Hmmm, that is a very creative proposal, young lady! I'll have to think about it, OK? In the meantime you should talk with your parents. Since you're a student and under fourteen years old, you must have their written permission to work. Why don't you bring your mother with you on next week's visit and we'll discuss it further," he said, signaling me to sit in his chair and tied the bib around my neck. "Now, let's get to those teeth."

I was so excited. When he finished, not only did I not have any cavities, I now had a new job. I skipped all the way home anxious to tell *Mami*, Los *Abuela*, and *Papito* when he got home tonight. I skipped into the kitchen yelling, "*Mami, Mami*, guess what? I found a job. I'm going to be Dr. Green's dental assistant." I blurted out the whole conversation word for word without taking a breath.

"Goodness, Raquel, what are you talking about? Young girls don't work. They go to school and get good grades.

After graduation they get married and have children," *Abuela* said.

Mami added, "Not quite, *Abuela*, this young girl, will graduate high school, then go to *la universidad* and then get married and have children, right, *Mija!*"

"That's right, *Mami*, but college is very expensive so I'll have to work and I can make better money in a dentist's office than at the five-n-dime-store, so I'll take the job, right!" Without taking another breath I continued.

"Besides, *Mami*, he wants to help the Spanish-speaking people and it's a good clean job and it's really close and he'll train me to make fillings, and even give our family a discount. You approve of that, don't you? Dr. Green wants us to go together next week so he can discuss it with you. Dr. Green even agreed to teach me to be a dental assistant so I can make even more money for college. Oh yes, and you and *Papito* have to sign a letter."

Mami's response was simple. "It's out of the question, Raquel and that's that!"

"Why is it out of the question?"

"Because, young lady! . . ."

Recognizing that glare in her eyes, I backed down a little.

"Hmph," I said as I walked away, muttering to myself. "We'll see about that, wait till I talk with *Papito!*"

That evening around the dinner table, everybody had an opinion about my new job. Of course, they all agreed with *Mami*, who stuck to her guns—"School, school, school, that is your job, young lady, to get a good education!" Sure, I thought to myself, what about my second job as your personal maid. If I work you'll have to pitch in a little extra at your least favorite things, like cooking and cleaning, right!

Abuela repeated over and over. "Girls your age don't work, they stay *en la casa.*"

"*La educación,*" *Abuelo* said emphatically, "that's what's important now." Sylvia chimed in her two cents worth saying, "*Por que?* Why do you want to work if you don't have to, *nena. Estas loca?* Just get smart enough to find a good husband and then let him take care of you." Venus chimed in, "Now that's a good idea, Sylvia."

It's the first time I ever heard Venus agree with Sylvia.

"Dina, Amorcito," Papito interrupted, "We should consider ourselves lucky that she even wants to work and earn money. Most kids in this neighborhood just want to do drugs and hang out on the streets and get into trouble."

All heads turned toward him.

"Not only that, *imaginate,* it was she who came up with the idea to help Dr. Green get new customers. That's very creative, don't you think, *querida?"*

"Si, *Papito,* that's what Dr. Green said too, it's a very creative proposal."

The family debate continued right through dessert and the end result was the same; *Mami* and *Abuela* won out.

"School is your only job now, young lady, *punto!"*

So, of course, I decided to take matters into my own hands. The next day, instead of hanging out in the schoolyard with my friends, I sneaked out and walked by Dr. Green's office so I could speak with him.

"I have another idea, Dr. Green, how about if you clean *Papito's* teeth for free or a big discount? This way you'll both get to know each other and it would give me time to find you some of those new clients and also allow *Papito* and me more time to work on persuading *Mami* and *Abuelita* to let me take the job?"

"Wow, young lady, you're really serious about this, aren't you?" Dr. Green exclaimed.

"Oh yes, I'm serious. I just need time to make it work. It's a perfect job for me."

For weeks I begged, cajoled and pleaded with *Mami* and *Abuela*, while secretly working on finding Dr. Green new clients. Each day after school I'd visit one of my school friends' homes and talk to their parents about Dr. Green. I already had Rosemarie and her grandmother, and *La Madrina* in

Apartment 8, and Brenda and her parents. I was up to seven families already, and they had lots of kids, not to mention aunts and uncles and cousins. Every day, as soon as I got home from school, I brought up the subject before doing my homework and during dinner. My constant badgering finally paid off, and after a month, I wore *Mami* down. She acquiesced, but of course, there were conditions. I'd have to give up time at the PAL and playing with friends, I had to keep my grades at a minimum of a B-plus level, and I couldn't miss any school.

"Sure, sure, don't worry, *Mami*, I can do this," was my reply. Of course, getting sick is not something one can control, but I was determined—no colds for me, *punto!*

In retrospect, *Mami* and *Abuela* were right about school. That's why many Hispanics migrated to the United States— for a better life, and a better life was attained through a good education. *Mami* may have not been the best "housekeeper" but she was very clear about the need for a good education. And in my case, where college seemed unaffordable, I had to at least be excellent and graduate high school with good grades, so getting a good education had to be my most important responsibility. As far as *Abuela* was concerned, I would be the first female in the family to graduate high school, a very great achievement in her eyes.

I agreed to all the terms *Mami* made, and the next day we went together to get fitted for my two new white uniforms, which Dr. Green paid for. I especially loved wearing the nurse's cap, though the sensible flat oxford walking shoes, which looked like a white version of the grandma shoes Dona Provi wore, were even uglier than my Buster Browns. But, I was too excited about earning my own money to complain about ugly shoes, and I must admit, they were comfortable. I guess that's why they were so ugly.

My first day of work was so exciting. I looked like a professional nurse all dressed up in my white uniform with my cap on. I arrived at the office thirty minutes early so I could set up the desk the way I wanted. I looked at the appointment book and noticed that we had four clients coming in, and they were all Spanish-speaking, which means I had brought them in. Not bad for our first night and there were also some appointments scheduled for Saturday too.

The first client was our tenant, Sylvia. I had to hand it to her; she was a tease and a pest sometimes, but here she was—being a good friend my first day on the new job. She was scheduled for a cleaning, her first cleaning in the U.S. Imagine that, she'd been here more than five years and still hadn't had her teeth cleaned. Poor Dr. Green!

After I checked the list of scheduled appointments for that night, I went in to make sure that the room was prepared with all the instruments in their place. Dr. Green had given me a two-day training session already, so I knew how to sterilize the instruments, make the silver that he used for cavities, set up his tray, and prepare the room after each patient left.

The previous Saturday, I also practiced with *Papito*, who gave up working in his store that day so I could be really prepared on my first day of work. He was so patient with me and kept smiling and saying, "*Que bien, Mija*, I'm proud." I made him come in and sit down in the reception area. Then I called and brought him into Dr. Green's workroom, seated him in the special chair and tied the bib around his neck. *Papito* let me practice about ten times till I got it just right. He's the best stepfather in the world.

Sylvia arrived right on time. "*Hola querida*," she shouted, as if I were at the other end of the long hallway at home, "I'm here."

"*Sylvia, hola.* Please, *sientate.*" I responded, pointing her toward a seat.

As I picked up the clipboard with the forms for her to fill out, I noticed she was dressed to the nines, as if she were going dancing and not to a dentist's office. Her make-up was perfect, including her bright red lipstick, which would have to be wiped off. She wore a tight navy blue dress with a low cut neckline showing off her cleavage, something both she and *Mami* loved to do. And, would you believe, she had on her high-heeled ankle strapped dancing shoes. Good heavens! Oh well, Dr. Green was a bachelor, and Sylvia would be Sylvia. She sat down, took off her gloves and kept smiling at me proudly.

"*Que linda ju look in dat juniform, nena.*"

I walked over and gave her a form to fill out.

"*Hay pero nena, ju hav to elp mi,*" she said in her thick accent and handed me the pen and clipboard.

So I sat next to her and translated everything that was asked in the form, her name, address and telephone, etc. This was easy since I knew most of the answers, but in order to practice, I asked the questions anyway, she answered in Spanish and I filled out the form in English. I made a mental note to ask future new clients to arrive a little earlier in order to make time to fill out the forms and still get them seated when Dr. Green was ready for them.

When it was time for Sylvia to be brought in, she started giggling uncontrollably. I couldn't get her to calm down. Then I sat her in the chair and she wouldn't let go of my hands, so I couldn't do my work. It's my first day on the job and she's the one who's nervous. I held her hand until Dr. Green walked in and I introduced her. He uttered the words I'd taught him with his own unique accent in his deep voice. "*Hola Sylvia, welcome to mi officeena.*"

She looked at him, smiled broadly and let go of my hand, forgetting me instantly.

"You have a beautiful smile," he said.

I could see the goose bumps on her arms. After all, he was a man, and a good-looking one too, and that's all Sylvia needed to help her relax. I put on her bib, presented the tray to Dr. Green for inspection, and while he selected his first tool, I placed the suction tube in Sylvia's mouth. It was weird looking into someone's mouth, especially someone you knew. I saw their teeth, their pink gums and their throat, and then there's all the bleeding. I wondered what it would be like with a patient who had bad breath, and I couldn't wait to get a patient that needed a cavity filled so I could blend the amalgam for someone's cavity. No such luck with Sylvia, though; it took Dr. Green the full hour to get her teeth cleaned, but she had no cavities. Even though she was a little sore afterwards she just kept smiling shamelessly at Dr. Green.

When Sylvia left, Don and Doña Jimenez, the *bodega* store owners, arrived. Great, his teeth were bad, so I knew I'd be making the amalgam mix tonight for sure. Unfortunately, I had to make it three times before I got it right.

We ended up working an hour later than planned, so Dr. Green walked me home. He always took an evening constitutional walk to clear his head, just like *Abuelo* did. *Mami* was not pleased about this because I still had to do my homework, but when I explained that I had already done most of it during my recess time, she nodded her approval.

When I got my first thirty dollars paycheck, which was fourteen dollars more than I used to make at McCrory's Five-N-Dime store, I went straight to the bank and opened a savings account. I deposited ten dollars for my college fund and five dollars for my voice classes. Then I put aside the five dollars for the household fund. With the last ten dollars I could buy material to sew my new clothes, have ice cream sundaes on a weekday basis as well as on Sunday, if I felt like it. I also decided to splurge on everyone. I bought *Abuela* her favorite *Agua de Florida* cologne and lemon verbena bath soap for *Mami* at the *botánica*. I also got tobacco for *Papito* and *Abuelo* and I even gave Venus one dollar. I was so proud of myself.

As it turned out I worked for Dr. Green for over four years, and eventually he trained me to be a full-fledged dental assistant. I learned the names of all of the instruments and the teeth, how to take X-rays, and did the teeth cleaning process myself. I also learned how to do the weekly accounting records and invoicing, although most of the Hispanic clients paid in cash.

Little did I know at the time that some day the skills I learned at Dr. Green's office as a dental assistant would help me support my family during a difficult time. Nor did I know that because of that job, the seeds of my entrepreneurial spirit had begun to blossom.

9

TITI MARÍA'S HEAVEN

*T*iti María's dream of finally returning to Puerto Rico came true the summer I became twelve. It was 1957 and Elvis Presley, whom everybody drooled over but me, was shaking up a storm on the Ed Sullivan Show with his latest hit, "You Ain't Nothing but A Hound Dog." The Russians had sent Sputnik out into the universe and Margaret Chase Smith, the only woman in Congress, was bravely challenging MaCarthy's tactics against Hollywood.

Back on Beck Street, *Titi* and *Abuela*, who for years secretly played *la bolita* (the numbers game) had finally won really big. Big enough for two round-trip tickets to Puerto Rico for an eight-week summer visit. My graduation present for completing the 6th grade with good marks was that I was to accompany *Titi María* on this momentous trip to *La Isla del Encanto*. At last I'd see with my own four eyes this magical place I'd heard about every day of my life. Finally I'd see and hear the palm trees sway, gaze at the gorgeous turquoise-colored ocean, eat mangoes right from the trees and meet my Island family. Wow! I'd prayed for a trip to Puerto Rico almost every night of my life, and now thanks to *la bolita* my prayers had been answered.

Abuela, Mami and *Titi Maria* worried a lot about the gangs and the deteriorating neighborhood we lived in, which became worse during the summers. Usually I spent the summers in Brooklyn, with my favorite cousin Gladys, where it was safer. I called her my *prima-hermana*, which means sister-cousin because she was the only real friend I had in the Ortiz family so far, and she was my cousin, so I gave her this special status. Gladys was toasted as being the most beautiful of the girl cousins on my father's side of the family. She had huge chestnut colored eyes underneath fanlike eyelashes, with unblemished toffee colored skin. She never got pimples. After *Mami*, she had the most beautiful graceful hands, with long fingertips and nails that were always manicured with mother-of-pearl nail polish. Like me, Gladys did all the cleaning at her house too, but no matter how hard she worked her nails were always perfect. Her mother *Titi Doris* was adamant about her being a feminine young lady and made sure Gladys was always groomed impeccably.

We met at the home of *Titi Lila,* another of *Papi Angel's* eight siblings, during the annual Ortiz family gathering. This was the only family event I was invited to and ironically neither my brothers nor *Papi Angel* attended. I guess he wasn't that interested in getting to know me or having me get to know my brothers. Oh well, I just put it out of my mind. I had a wonderful Papito, so there.

Gladys and I fell in love with each other instantly and decided right then and there that we'd be best friends. We even determined we'd be each other's maid-of-honor when we got married and godparents to our first born children. Imagine making such momentous decisions right on the spot. From then on we always sought each other out at the family parties, and visited each other almost every other weekend and in the summers. When I told Gladys about my good news we were both excited about my adventure yet a little sad because we wouldn't see each other that summer. I promised to write her every week to tell her about all of my adventures.

Titi Maria had so many things she wanted to teach me about Puerto Rico. She wanted me to get connected to my roots, to see and experience the intense beauty up close. Most important of all she wanted me to understand that what I saw of Puerto Ricans in the South Bronx and New York City neighborhoods was just part of a bigger story. "Puerto Ricans on *La Isla* are the majority, she said. They work in the fields and the factories, in the government, in the hospitals and they go to school and to church with their families. They have beach picnics and lots of outdoor fun filled with delicious food and music. Yes, it's true they sit on their front porches rocking and fanning themselves and the men play dominoes just like in the Bronx, but they don't have gangs like we do here. Kids worked in the fields or had chores at home, so they didn't have much time to get into trouble. That's the way it was back then, though it's changed a great deal now.

All I could think about was spending two months in Puerto Rico. That's eight whole weeks, a wonderfully long time to be in *Titi María's* heaven. My goodness, was I lucky or what!

First we planned to visit a cousin's secluded *finca* (farm) in the hills of *Manati*. Then after a few weeks we'd visit another aunt, whom *Mami* said was well-to-do." I couldn't quite figure out what "well-to-do" meant. It sounded like she was in-between something, like she had lots of money but not tons of it, yet she wasn't poor like us. Oh, well, I'd find out soon enough. All I knew was that the "well-to-do" *Titi Violeta* lived in a fancy house on a farm in *Aguadilla* and that she had three living rooms. This I had to see.

I was heartbroken that *Abuelita* couldn't come with us, because the school where she worked making lunch had summer classes scheduled. It's not fair, she gets lucky by winning at *la bolita* and then she can't have the fun of going back home with us because of work. I tried not to act too happy about my good fortune, but then *Abuela* thought I didn't want to go and her feelings were hurt. *"No quieres ir Raquel?"* Once I heard that I just let my joy shine. I talked and daydreamed about my trip to *La Isla* all day. Sometimes I even sang *En Mi Viejo San Juan,* a beautiful melancholic ode to a place I loved though I hadn't seen it yet.

The only one almost as happy about my trip besides me that is, was Venus, though she acted like she was jealous. "I wouldn't go to Puerto Rico if they paid me," she'd say, "I heard they have flying cockroaches there." But I knew it was all an act. Secretly Venus was really thrilled, because she'd have *Papito* all to herself. Anyway, nothing could mar my joy about this wonderful adventure I'd always dreamed about. So I ignored her and focused on what to pack: not that I had much. *Mami* said she'd take me shopping on Saturday to buy a new bathing suit and some shorts, but *Titi María* said, "Don't buy anything here, wait till we get to Puerto Rico so you can get the styles that young girls are wearing on *la isla.* "A Puerto Rican bathing suit, how exciting, I thought. Are they different? Then immediately I began thinking about the contrasts between the Island and New York. I don't know how I managed to finish school that June. Between studying for end-of-the-year exams and daydreaming about the trip, *Mami* said I was like a whirling dervish, whatever that is.

Finally the day came for us to drive to Idewild Airport in Long Island City and take the Eastern Airlines flight to Puerto Rico. In spite of what *Titi María* said about waiting to shop for clothes in Puerto Rico, *Mami* made me a new pants outfit to travel in. It was a white seersucker cotton shirt and pedal-pusher pants set. I tied a small orange scarf around my neck and carried a big straw bag filled with my books, personal things and gift boxes from *Mami* for my Puerto Rican family.

Though I'd never been on an airplane before, I was too

excited to be nervous, but this was *Titi María's* first flight and she was so scared her hands trembled. *"Yo prefiero los barcos,"* she'd mutter to herself at least ten times a day, though it was loud enough for all of us to hear. She preferred boats because that is how she, *Mami, Abuelo* and *Abuela* came to the New York from Puerto Rico in March of 1945. *Mami* was about three months pregnant with me at the time they left Puerto Rico with my two brothers. My natural birth father, Angel, was in the 65th Infantry Army Regiment at the time, so he would join us later. I always wished *Mami* had waited a little longer so I could have been born in Puerto Rico, but unfortunately at the time I couldn't voice that opinion.

The minute we got to the airport, *Titi María* grabbed onto my hand for dear life and didn't let go until we landed at San Juan's International Airport. I had expected to see blue skies right away but we arrived at nighttime so it was pitch dark outside. There were palm trees and the airport was open and airy, not enclosed like in New York. *Tio Carlos, Titi Andrea* and my cousin *Puchi* met us at the airport. In Puerto Rico it's the custom for everyone to be met at the airport. Even if you're one person, half-a-dozen people come to pick you up. The minute they see you they start calling your name, waving and jumping up and down so you can see them in the crowd. Of course, when they yelled for *Titi María,* almost all the older ladies responded, as just about every female in Puerto Rico has the name Maria in there somewhere. When we finally got out with our luggage we were hugged and kissed, and there were squeals and tears and more hugs. It was so exciting! I felt famous like a movie star, especially since they were people whom I'd never seen before.

We drove to *Tio Carlos's finca* in *Manati* that night. It was pitch black outside, so once we left the airport there was nothing much to see but the moon and what seemed like a zillion stars, both shining brighter than in the Bronx. And, for the first time, I heard the strange and wonderful music of the small island frog, *el coquí*, thousands of them whistling in the night, "*coquí, coquí, coquí.*" I lay back to look out of the rear window at the shadows the palm trees made in the night and was soon lulled to sleep by the *coquí* symphony.

When we arrived there were more people at the house, cousins, aunts, neighbors all waiting to greet us. And there was food. Thank goodness, my stomach was growling so loud everyone could hear it. There were potato dumplings stuffed with tasty ground ham and cheese called *croquetas* and homemade *limonada.*

"They're lemons from our very tree!" said *Tio Carlos.*

As soon as I ate, my eyes got droopy again so they put me right to sleep. I had a room all to myself with a dark wooden four-post bed over which hung a sheer white net, like a bride's veil. It's called a *mosquitero* to keep the mosquitoes from biting you in the middle of the night.

I was asleep before my head hit the pillow and slept like a baby. I awoke to the sound of the roosters squealing *cukurucukoo* very early in the morning, but went right back to sleep. At about 9:00AM I awoke again, this time scratching myself all over. When I looked at myself I let out a loud scream and everybody came running. "*Muchacha, que pasa,* what's wrong?" they all said. Then *Titi María* let out a yelp too. "*Diós mio,*" she said looking at my arms and legs. I looked like a hairless chicken with goose bumps all over, only these were red little spots. It was so hot that I took my clothes off in the middle of the night, then twisted and turned around so much, that the mosquito net came off. I looked like I had the measles. "*Sangre dulce*" *Titi Andrea* said, "she has sweet blood just what the mosquitoes love." Welcome to the Island *Raquelita*. I took a shower and then *Titi María* put tons of pink salve all over my legs, arms, back, chest, neck, ears, face, and even my *fondillo*. I even had bites on my backside and fingers. It was awful. *Titi* giggled as she smothered me in the pink lotion muttering, *sangre dulce* over and over. When the lotion dried it looked like pink chalk. They dressed me in a very loose white nightgown that was soft and sheer so I couldn't feel it on my skin.

At last it was time for breakfast. I had oatmeal and *leche* with a drop of *café* just like *Abuela* makes for me with *tostada criolla,* delicious fresh baked French bread that is flattened out like a pancake and smothered with fresh farm butter. It was so good I forgot all about my bites, even the ones I was sitting on. After stuffing myself, I went out onto the porch with *Puchi.* "What happened to the *coquís,"* I asked?

"Oh, they only come out at night after sunset."

The sun is brighter on the island and the sky is a deep cerulean blue speckled with cotton-puff clouds. Though it's hot and humid, there is always a breeze and the air smells fresh, instead of dank and dirty, like in the city. I took in a few deep breaths and noticed that the air didn't hurt your nostrils like the cold winter air up north. I looked around and saw that there was a hammock and many rocking chairs on the porch, six or seven rockers. And, to my delight, here was a second hammock between two trees in front of the house.

"What's that sweet smell?"

"Mango trees", replied Puchi.

"Mangos, real mangos on the tree?" I exclaimed! "That's my favorite fruit, but we only get them in the summer in New York and they're very expensive because they're imported, from here."

I immediately skipped toward the tree and climbed onto the hammock. As I lay down, I took in a deep slow breath and filled my nostrils with mango sweetness. The aroma was much stronger here underneath this tree than at the counters in *La Marketa.* 'Would it taste sweeter too,' I wondered? Gently swaying from side to side I looked up through the leaves at the brilliant blue sky and soon dozed off again.

I awoke two hours later thinking that if this kept up I

wouldn't see much of the Island. But, first things first. I smelled something delicious in the air. It must be lunchtime! *Titi María* said I was getting accustomed to the weather and it would take a few more days before the sleepiness wore off. The humidity made my hair really curly, so she braided it real tight pulling back my forehead as if she wanted to stretch my skin. She told me to wear shorts and a sleeveless blouse and I donned the brand new white tennis shoes that *Mami* bought me at Woolworth's department store.

We had avocado and cheese sandwiches with *sopa de pollo*. It's too hot to eat chicken soup I said. *Titi María* replied, "it's good for you to eat soup in hot weather it levels your temperature." This sounded like another one of those adult claims. I didn't believe her, but I was hungry as usual, so I ate it. It was delicious just like *Abuela*'s.

After lunch *Puchi* and I went to feed the animals. I noticed he was barefoot, so I took off my white sneakers too and we walked barefoot all day long. I loved the feel of the dewy wet grass under my feet and toes, but when we had to walk on gravely surfaces it hurt. It didn't seem to bother *Puchi*, though, I guess he was used to it.

They had chickens and roosters and rabbits, lots of them, all white. It's so cute the way the bunnies sit and wiggle their noses all day long. Behind the *finca* there was a railroad track that we crossed to gather food for the rabbits. There wasn't another house around for miles, just green pastures and lots of mango trees, palm trees with coconuts and plantain trees as far as you could see. But I was puzzled. Where was the water? Puerto Rico was an Island, surrounded by water, why couldn't I see the ocean?

What I didn't know was that *Manati* is a beautiful farm town on the northern part of the Island heading west about 48 miles outside of San Juan where the airport is located. It was inland enough so that we couldn't see the water from our farm. When we returned from feeding the animals I asked *Titi María*, "I want to see *la playa, Titi*, when can we go to the beach?" That night at dinner it was decided we would go to the beach the next day. Imagine going to the beach in the middle of the week. Back home we only went on the weekend, even though we weren't in school.

Luquillo Beach was so different from Orchard Beach in the Bronx that all I could do was say, Wow! It was shaped like a horseshoe and the water was the most vibrant shade of turquoise I had ever seen. By the shore the water was clear and pale, and you could see your toes in it, but the color deepened as it stretched out toward the horizon. The beach was lined with palm trees, tall ones and short ones, so you could hide from the scorching mid-day sun. The sand was very fine and the color of linen. There was a section for bathrooms where you could change clothes when you arrived, and outdoor showers by the parking lot so you could rinse the sand off your body before you left the beach. I wondered why didn't they have that at Orchard Beach in the Bronx. Vendors with glistening skin periodically strolled by yelling *cerveza fría,* coka cola or *coquítos,* a coconut-flavored sherbet that sold for ten cents. At the food stand they sold hot dogs, chips, meat-dumplings called *alcapurrias, bacalao frito,* fried codfish patties and cold coconut juice that you drank right out of the shell through a straw. We arrived early in the morning and set ourselves up right underneath a palm tree and stayed till the sun set.

The one thing that *Luquillo* Beach had in common with Orchard Beach was that there was music and dancing. Young cute guys with sweaty bodies played conga drums and scraped their *guiros,* gourds with ridges that the player scrapes against with an instrument that looks like a hair pick. Clusters of people danced to the rhythmic beat of the African *plena* while the on-lookers clapped to the syncopation of the *clave* sticks. One, two, three . . . four-five, one, two, three . . . four-five.

I was too anxious to get to the water to watch the musicians, so I dropped my packages and raced toward it. I stopped just as we hit the edge of the water and put my toe in. I couldn't believe it. It was warm, almost like bath water when you fill up the tub. When I tested the water at Orchard Beach I'd immediately get goose bumps all over my body because it was so icy cold. I rarely got in. I wondered how it could be that the same body of water, the Atlantic Ocean, was a dark blue-gray color and freezing ice cold in New York, even in the summer, and in Puerto Rico it was a light blue-green color, warm, calm and inviting.

Slowly I tiptoed in and let the water envelop me. It was cool enough to be refreshing but once you were totally dunked in it, it was like a warm soothing bath. For the first time in my life I put my head underneath the water. It was refreshing. I sat with the water up to my neck allowing the gentle warm waves to wash over me as I stared out at the line where the ocean and sky kiss. That was my first experience with bliss. Today, whenever I close my eyes in meditation and take myself there, I experience it in exactly the same sublime way.

The next exciting adventure on my Puerto Rican trip was the visit to the house of the "well-to-do" family in *Aguadilla,* on the northwest tip of the Island. Even *Titi María* was anxious to see the living room behind glass doors that her sister *Titi Violeta* wrote her about. The house was big and white and sat on the mountaintop. It was covered with shiny blue Spanish tiles on the roof and had a big archway entrance. The best part was the terrace on all four sides of the house, also speckled with rocking chairs and hammocks, and surrounded by tall leafy palm trees waving in the wind. It looked like the hand-painted picture postcards they sold at the airport newsstand.

My first impression of *Titi Violeta* and my *prima Dolores* as they greeted us underneath the main entrance of their mountaintop home, was how fancy their clothes were for people who lived on a farm, though this was a special occasion for all of us. *Titi Violeta* and *Dolores* wore white linen dresses with lavender colored flowers delicately embroidered on the bodice and hem, and a matching long ribbon at the waist. As it turns out they dressed like this every day, always wearing white and oftentimes looking like twins, only one was big and the other small. *Titi Violeta* was a seamstress and made and embroidered all their clothes, and believe me, they had plenty of dresses, which is all they ever wore. You see, they didn't work the farm, they just owned it. They both loved jewelry too. *Titi Violeta* wore a cameo broach at her neck, which she often said *Dolores* would inherit someday, like I was to inherit *Titi María's* emerald stone that she kept inside a tiny silk purse of the same color. They reminded me of the English ladies I'd read about in "Wuthering Heights" and "Jane Eyre".

My cousin *Dolores* had a gold bracelet with a heart-shaped charm and an emerald at the tip of the heart. I felt sure we'd be great friends, because we had the emerald birthstone in common, meaning we were both born in May.

"How lucky you are to have an emerald." I said. "One day I'll have one too. *Titi María* promised that when I turn eighteen and graduate high school, she'll give me the emerald stone she keeps in a little silk purse around her neck, like an heirloom. It's her special protection and she only takes it off when she bathes."

"Well, I have mine now and it's not in a little silk purse, it's on my arm in my 18-karat gold bracelet and I wear it *todos los dias* too", she retorted, arrogantly shaking her arm in my face.

As the week passed I began to realize that I didn't like my cousin *Dolores* that much. She was spoiled, unfriendly and always showing off her dress, her toys, her room and especially her jewelry. I didn't have much fun playing with her either. All she did was talk about her things, 'I have this and I have that, we do this or we go there,' constantly showing me what was in her drawers or closets, or the boxes underneath her bed. She always spoke in an angry tone, which I found annoying. What did she have to be angry about? Actually I liked *Puchi* more. He was friendly and warm and loved to play in the grass, rock on the hammock, and eat mangoes and frozen ice cones. *Puchi* would ask me to say words in English, then he'd repeat them with his very thick accent and then laugh at himself uncontrollably.

One day *Dolores* was unexpectedly nice to me and said I could wear the gold bracelet with the emerald charm. I was so thrilled because I admired that bracelet and thought she was finally being nice to me. I wore the bracelet happily and stared at it all day long, both to enjoy it and make sure it didn't fall off. The next day, right in front of her mother, she yelled and pointed at me, "Oh there it is, I thought it was lost. How did you get it," grabbing my arm to show her mother.

"*Pero, Dolores*, you lent it to me remember", I said, tears welling up in my eyes.

Titi Violeta came over and shook me from head to toe by the shoulders yelling. 'Why do I always cry when I'm angry.'

"*Nena*, young girls *no roban*".

"But, I didn't steal it *Titi Violeta, Dolores* said I could borrow it for a day or two before I leave."

I looked over at Dolores who had this innocent look on her face like she didn't know what I was talking about.

"*Mentirosa*, don't lie, *Dolores* is not allowed to do that. Then, she slapped me.

"*Vete*, go to your room until dinnertime".

I was so angry and ashamed. I went to the porch instead and cried for a long time. The mosquitoes didn't even bother me nor did the *coquís'* song drown out my anger and sorrow.

Later, when I recovered from my crying, I quietly tiptoed into the special living room behind the glass doors, on the opposite side of the house. I gently slid the door open just enough to shimmy in and I sat myself right in the middle of the white silk brocade sofa and rocked back and forth, thinking, Humph, let them find me right here. Who cares?

Who ever heard of a living room behind glass doors that you don't even sit in, except maybe in a museum, it's dumb. I pouted and left the sliding door open so the humidity and the mosquitoes could get in too, even if they bit me. After a while of rocking I got drowsy and laid down, shoes and all, on the white fancy sofa.

Suddenly I heard yelling in my dream and jumped right up. It wasn't a dream it was *Titi Violeta* once again screaming at me, with *Titi María, Tio Carlos and Dolores* standing behind her glaring at me.

"*Quitate*, get off of that sofa! How dare you, first the bracelet, then the special living room, *Diós Mio*."

Titi María, who had just returned from shopping, asked *Titi Violeta* to stop screaming at me. Next thing we knew they were screaming at each other in Spanish, their hands flying all over the place, talking so fast, that no one could interrupt them. *Tio Carlos* threw his hands up and walked away. Dolores came over and yanked me off the sofa and began dusting it off as if there were a stain on it or something. Finally, *Titi María* said "*Nos vamos,* pack your things Raquel, we're going back to *Manati,* right now come on."

That was it, we packed and left. While in the taxi *público* driving back I explained to *Titi* what happened with the bracelet. She said, "Don't worry, *Mija* that's why I rarely visit my sister. *Violeta* has always been a little stuck up *y esa Dolores* is a spoiled brat too, and now that they have money, it's even worse. We'll have more fun in *Manati.* This weekend we'll go to a phosphorescent bay on the southwest coast of the Island called *La Parguera.* On a moonless night we'll go out onto the lake in a dinghy and in the pitch dark of night we'll scoop water up in our hands and see it glow with little stars. *Es bello* it's very beautiful." I put my head in *Titi's* lap and listened to the *coquis* all the way back to *Manati.* I couldn't wait to see *Puchi* and take off my shoes, walk on the shore and enjoy the water with stars with him.

I spent the rest of the summer walking barefoot with *Puchi* to find food for the rabbits or reading my book while swinging on the hammock. When I got hungry, I'd climb up, pick a couple of mangos, peel and eat them right there. I'd get my hands and mouth all gushy and messy, but I always kept tissues in my pockets so I could clean them without having to leave my favorite spot underneath the mango tree in front of the *Manati finca.* The fruit I liked besides mangos were *quenepas,* (in Cuba they call them *mamonsillos)* the size of a grape with a green shell that you broke into with your teeth and then sucked on the fuzzy bittersweet fruit that surrounded the pit. I'd eat dozens of them at a time. There were all kinds of delicious food to savor; cod fish salad with avocado, *yucca* and plantains, called *serenata;* rabbit stew that tasted like tender chicken, and homemade coconut ice cream for dessert. Every weekend we'd go to the beach and I got so dark they called me *la negrita.* This time it was a compliment.

Experiencing Puerto Rico was the most wonderful summer of my childhood. At first I hardly missed *Mami* and *Papito* and my grandparents. It was the best time. Years later, as an adult, just thinking about it brings back the sweet smell of fresh picked mangoes, the salty humid scent of the ocean, the swishing sound of palm tress flowing in the wind and the cacophony of the *coquís* nightly symphony. I love that sound so much that I almost always call my friends and family in Puerto Rico in the evening, so I can hear the *coquis* singing in the background.

Before I realized it, the eight weeks were almost over and *Titi María* had already begun to pack my things and cook special delicacies like white and molasses-colored grated coconut balls, and other goodies, to bring back to our family in the Bronx. Though I was feeling a little anxious to get home and share all my stories with the family, I also felt a sadness begin to take over at the thought of having to leave this beautiful place. I sensed something wasn't quite right, but I couldn't put my finger on it yet.

On the morning of our departure everyone piled into

the car, each of us looking a little withdrawn. *Puchi* was frowning and grumpy because he had to wear shoes. He hated wearing shoes even for school, but at least then he could wear sandals. Today he wore his Sunday best, black laced shoes and socks and long black pants with a white linen *guayabera* shirt.

When we arrived at the Puerto Rico airport I noticed there wasn't as much luggage going back with us as when we flew down to the Island, even though there were two new shopping bags for me to take as carry-on luggage. Puerto Ricans are famous for their shopping bags and super big suitcases because we always bring back goodies for everyone from the Island. Of course, we weren't allowed to bring fresh fruit or plantains, but we could bring packaged goods: things like coffee and special little bite-sized crackers called "*100to En Boca*" (one-hundred-mouthfuls). They look like the crackers you put in clam chowder, only they're puffier and sweet and Puerto Ricans just love them. We could also bring cooked foods like rice and beans and *pasteles*. It seemed to all of us that when these foods are cooked on the Island they taste much better.

So, we tearfully boarded the airplane headed to New York that Puerto Ricans referred to as *la guagua aerea*. Islanders called it "the air bus" because there were so many daily flights to and from Puerto Rico and the US, like a bus service, filled to the brim with Puerto Rican families, their kids, toys, and a couple of shopping bags stuffed with goodies for their mainland families. On the one hand we're happy to be going back to our families in the States, and on the other, we're terribly sad to leave our hearts and souls behind on *La Isla*. Now, I too felt the same way. Since my first trip to Puerto Rico I have always felt like I have one foot on the island and the other in the States, split right down the middle between two cultures, two countries, two lives. It's a feeling that's stayed with me forever, a feeling that is true for all *Boricuas*. No matter where we are and what we do, a piece of us always remains behind. That is the sentiment in the lyrics of the song *"En Mi Viejo San Juan."*

For me, that schizophrenic ache began when *Titi María* told me she was not returning to the Bronx with me. *Titi* had decided to live out the rest of her days in her homeland.

"Yo me quedo en mi Patria," she said hugging me tightly. I was to travel home alone. I was shocked. My chest began heaving in and out and I couldn't breathe. I didn't want her to stay, so I held onto her clothes for dear life. She too held on tightly until it was time to board and she peeled my fingers away from her skirt. She knelt down and looked into my eyes, placed two shopping bags in my hands and then slipped something in my pocket. She hugged me tightly once again and whispered in my ear, "Promise me you won't open this, pointing to my pocket, until after the plane takes off. *Prométemelo!"* I shook my head yes emphatically, turned and walked through the gate toward the plane, tears gushing down my face, my shoulders shaking uncontrollably.

I sat in my seat and turned to look out of the small window. *Titi María* was still waving goodbye. Again the tears welled up. Tears of sadness for my loss and tears of joy for *Titi María.* I now felt the opposite of bliss—a deep heavy ache in my heart as if an anvil were pressed against my chest. I was leaving behind my *Titi María* and the Puerto Rico I had fallen in love with. I wanted to run off the plane into her arms, but the doors had been shut and the plane left the gate.

Once the packages were all squashed underneath the seat and my seatbelt was tightly fastened, I opened the package in my pocket. I held my breath. Inside was the little silk purse that held the precious emerald stone, my heirloom. More tears flowed. *Titi's* whispered words echoed in my head. "Know that I'll always be with you. Remember when you really love someone, you think of what's best for them, even if that sometimes means being separated." And so, my first lesson in letting go took place as I boarded the plane that

would take me back to the South Bronx without my beloved
Titi María. My breathing calmed down as I realized that as
long as I had The Silk Purse, and as long as I kept her memory
in my heart, a part of *Titi María* would always be with me. I
remembered the look of joy on *Titi's* face as she said, "I'm
staying here," her eyes sparkling and her back even straighter
than usual. She had made the right decision, she was in
heaven, and for her, heaven was in Puerto Rico.

I tied the silk purse around my neck hiding it underneath
my blouse, then lay my head against the window and watched
Puerto Rico disappear into a tiny speck on the ocean. As we
cut through the clouds I felt as if God would appear through
the rays any moment. I closed my eyes and relived my first
trip to *La Isla del Encanto*.

I recalled *Titi María's* heaven, now mine too, where I
savored the sweet gooey mangoes, relished the spicy rabbit
stew with the garlicky *mofongo* and peacefully swayed on the
hammock reading every day. I relived carving my name
alongside my mother's and grandmother's, on that mango
tree. I savored my first moment of bliss on Luquillo Beach,
as I gazed out at that point where the ocean kisses the sky
and languidly swallows the brilliant orange sun.

As I began to think about the changes I would find at
home, I heard someone behind me ask the Stewardess about
the strange smell on board the plane. I shrank down in my
seat, hoping no one would realize it was the pungent crab
casseroles I had been entrusted with, and consold myself by
fondling my Silk Purse.

10

THE SECRET

It was the summer of 1958 and *Papito* had joined the throngs of Americans who were buying automobiles. His was a two-toned sea-foam green Buick, long, sleek, classy and shiny as new, though it was second-hand. Now on weekends we'd go visit friends and families living in the suburbs of New Jersey or Long Island. Venus and I sat in the back and had to be still. We weren't allowed to eat or drink anything lest we stain the matching sea-foam green upholstery. During the week, *Papito* parked the car in a garage, so if we went to the beach we still had to go via subway.

On this humid, ninety-degree New York summer day, the South Bronx was still and quiet. It was too hot and humid to jump rope or play handball. I was sitting on the front stoop reading, waiting for *Mami*, my sister, *La Comadre* and her four kids to come down so we could leave for Orchard Beach to dunk our overheated bodies in the cold Atlantic waters. I loved the ocean, even though the water was cold, it was so big it touched the other end of the world, and swished all the time, like my mind, in a constant state of movement—flowing, thinking, dreaming.

Our stoop was a special gathering place, especially in the summer, when it was hot enough for the kids and the grown-ups to sit around and relax. The men played dominoes and talked about news and politics. The women mended clothes or knit winter sweaters and, yes, talked about politics too sometimes, distractedly chiming in an opposing comment. Other times they sat quietly in each other's company, watching their kids play. The political conversations were often about the status of Puerto Rico: Should it become a state, stay as a commonwealth, or risk it all to become a sovereign nation? The men were for the status quo or statehood, and most of the women didn't have an opinion or felt it was best to leave well enough alone—status quo. These days, *Papito*'s favorite subject was Fidel Castro, a Cuban who was publicly challenging General Fulgencio Battista*'s* corrupt government. *Los Abuelo*s were the only ones who wanted independence for Puerto Rico, and *Papito* was pro the Cuban revolution. There was never total agreement on which way to go, but the discussions were passionate and fun to listen to though I didn't always understand their reasoning.

The rest of the kids hardly paid attention to these heated debates. Instead, like the adults, they divided themselves up by gender, the boys played baseball or free handball and the girls jumped rope or hopscotch and sang rhymes until it was time for our nightly bath and bed. During the day, though, the stoop was a peaceful, quiet place.

On this stifling morning, I had the stoop all to myself, peacefully sitting away from my big bossy family with no chores to do and eager to begin the new book I had borrowed from the public library, *A Tree Grows in Brooklyn* by Betty Smith. I knew *Mami* and *Madrina* and her brood would take a long time getting ready for our beach trip. I got my stuff together early and decided to wait for them downstairs, that way I wouldn't have to help dress the kids or make sandwiches for the beach. I couldn't wait to learn about the young girl in my book named Francie, who was about my age and lived not too far from where Gladys lived in the neighboring borough of Brooklyn. I wondered how old she would be. Did her family speak two languages like we did? What were her friends and family like? What was her favorite game? Did she play jacks, or like music and books like me?

My friends always made fun of me because I loved to read, especially on the front stoop. They didn't understand that there I had peace and quiet and *Mami* could still watch out for me, or call if she needed to. "There's *La Bookworm* at it again," they'd say, "doesn't she get bored?" It was the only thing they said about me that didn't bother me. When they called me "Skinny Minnie," I was mortified, wondering if I'd ever gain weight. Lord knows I ate enough. It seemed I was always hungry and always munching on something. I'd go on periodic eating binges—eating second servings of *arroz con pollo and beans* so I could gain weight, but it never stuck. I guess *Abuela* was right about that *gusano* (worm) in my stomach eating up everything I ingested. I didn't like that idea one bit. Wouldn't they be surprised if they could see my zaftig body now!

When they made fun of my curly kinky hair, I began pulling it into a super tight ponytail, hoping to straighten it out forever. No such luck! And to add insult to injury, I was also the only girl on the block, practically in the whole neighborhood, who wore glasses, so of course, they called me "four-eyes," which I didn't like either. But when they called me *La Bookworm,* I took it as a compliment, because it was a wonderful way to escape from chores and the dangerous city and I knew it would make me smarter one day.

I'm glad *Mami* encouraged me to read. Aside from the fact that I loved to read then, and still do, it was also the only time she left me alone. She was constantly on my case about everything—my chores around the house, watching over my little sister, the grocery list, the constant trips to the bodega, my homework, my hair, my clothes, the dog, my room, excuse me, our room. Give me a break!

Mother was *una romantica.* She loved romantic Gothic novels, Spanish poetry, museums, walking in the rain, window-shopping, and dancing *boleros* in the moonlight with *Papito.* If it were a choice between reading, visiting friends or going window-shopping, and cleaning house, she'd happily spend the day in her bedroom reading and leave the chores to *Abuela* and me. She'd often tell me, "Reading is my escape, *Mija,* it's how I keep romance in my life, you'll see." She had this little ditty about books that she constantly repeated. "If you can read, you can escape your reality and you can learn, if you can learn, you can write, and if you can write, you can share your ideas and make your dreams a reality."

Every year for Christmas, though our list was always short because money was tight, Venus and I could count on two gifts: a new Sunday dress and shoes, and, a new book. A big fat book like *Wuthering Heights* or *Gone with the Wind* that given all my homework, errands and chores, took me practically all year long to read. The surprise in these gifts was that we never knew the title of the book and we never saw the dress until that day. One year Venus and I got matching dresses with a mink collar and muff. The shoes, however, were always the same black patent leather Mary Janes, two sizes bigger than last year, so they'd last until next year. If we were lucky, meaning if *Papito* made good money, and we had truly been *nenitas buenas,* Santa would leave us good little girls a special present. Venus called these the "real Santa presents," like our first pair of ice skates or my Barbie Doll with a ponytail and eyeglasses. The others were "parent presents,"—"sensible instead of fun," she'd say. Smart girl, my little sister.

Every Sunday after dinner, Mother expected us to read passages from our books, and as if we didn't have enough homework, we also had to write a book report when we finished the book. The rule was no book report, no PAL or TV or playing on the stoop. *Mami* would check and grade them just like my English teacher, Mrs. MacCauley. Although I loved reading, I disliked the extra homework.

About a half-an-hour into my reading reverie on the front stoop, a very tall boy came onto the stoop. "Hey," he muttered as he walked past me. "Hey," I responded without looking up. A few minutes later he came back out, smiled from ear to ear and asked, "Hey, do you know which apartment Freddie lives in?" "No," I said, "we don't have a Freddie, we have a Frankie."

"Yeah, yeah, that's him, Frankie," he said enthusiastically.

"Oh sure," I got up and went into the hallway, saying, "He's my godmother's son, ring number eight."

As I walked into the tiny foyer, I noticed he was taller than *Papito*, who was exactly six feet. I pointed to the mailbox and the buzzer. Before I could press the button, the door buzzed, he pushed it open, grabbed my ponytail and shoved me into the inner hallway and into an alcove underneath the stairs. When he first walked in, he seemed friendly enough, but now his smile was more like a scowl. My heart skipped twenty beats and began thumping so loud I heard it in my ears. It reminded me of my first train ride with *Mami* and *Papito*; I was scared then and I was scared now. I opened my mouth to yell, but only a squeak came out. I, who could sing in three octaves along with Barbra Streisand and Xiomara Alfaro, now squealed like a mouse. I had lost my voice.

He covered my entire face with his hand, saying, "Do what I tell you or I'll cut you up and throw you in the garbage can." In his other hand was a knife. It was a little knife, like the one grandpa carried in his pocket to clean his fingernails,

but when he put it against my throat and grabbed my face
with his huge hand, it looked really big. I obeyed.

I started to pray in my head, "*Ay Diós, Mami*, please, please
come down the stairs now, *Mami*." We passed Door Number
4, my apartment, and continued up to the next floor, passing
numbers 5 and 6. No one was home on the third floor this
week. Mr. and Miss Eisen were at the Poconos and the
Sanchezes were on vacation in Puerto Rico. As we
approached the fourth flight of stairs, I could hear my
mother's voice coming out of *Madrina's* apartment. "Hurry
up, *avancen ninos*, or we'll lose the sun." *Madrina* had five
kids, so she always needed help getting ready to go to the
beach, or anywhere else, for that matter. Then I got this
crazy idea in my head. Sing, I thought, sing out loud. So, I
began singing *The autumn leaves, drift by my window, the autumn
leaves* . . . Imagine singing at a time like this, and a romantic
song no less. Even he stopped and stared at me for a quick
second. I usually sing when I'm lonely or depressed, but
when my life is in danger? I guess I hoped *Mami* would hear
me, open the door and take me out of this man's clutches.
No such luck! I could hear everyone in *La Comadre's* house
running around and yelling at each other. "Hurry up, we'll
lose the sun," "I don't wanna go to the beach today," and
"Finish your breakfast." There is no way they could hear me
singing.

He quickly came to his senses and covered my mouth
again, this time with a smelly handkerchief. I struggled to
release myself from his grasp but couldn't. He was too big
and strong. *God, why don't they teach girls how to box*, I thought,
*they teach boys how to fight and they teach us how to play with dolls
and cook*. Next, I wished I was fat, maybe then he wouldn't
have been able to hold on to me so well. We passed the
fourth floor and went up the small set of stairs that led to
the roof. The door, which was usually closed, was open. *Shit*,
I thought. It was a big heavy metal door that squeaked loudly
when you opened it, like the ones in monster movies. Had it

been closed someone might have heard it squeaking as he opened it. Again, bad luck.

He pushed me onto the roof, then stood me up on the ledge, making me look down. "If you do what I want, I won't throw you down." He was twice my size and dangled me over the ledge like a rag doll. No one was on the stoop. I saw the sharp points of the wrought-iron railing around our building and began trembling as I imagined myself skewered by them. I shook my head, frantically agreeing. I couldn't breathe, couldn't talk and couldn't scream.

He threw me in a corner onto the hot tar. It singed my legs. He opened his pants, pulled out his long dark ugly thing, and shoved it in my mouth then started jumping and bumping like a crazy man. I was choking and gagging but he kept thumping frantically. When he finally stopped bumping into my face, this slimy bitter liquid oozed into my mouth. He took the ugly thing out and slimy liquid spilled into my eyes, up my nose, all over my face, into my ears and down my neck. Then he calmed down for a minute though he didn't release his grip on me, while I wretched convulsively. After a few minutes, he wrapped his shirt over my mouth, turned me around, pulled up my dress, pulled down my panties and put his thing into my *culito*. As he started bumping against my behind, it felt as if he'd ripped open my *culito* and it broke. I felt myself go numb, then everything went black.

I awoke to the sounds of *Mami's* voice. "*Raquel, Raquel, Diós mio nena*, where are you, we're ready to go to *la playa*." I jumped up, then hunched over. I hurt everywhere, my head, my neck and my face, my legs and my ass. I peered around nervously. He was gone and my keys were by my feet. I picked them up, tiptoed down the stairs, quietly tiptoed into our apartment and headed towards the bathroom. I took off my panties ripped them up into shreds and threw them in the garbage. I washed my face and my behind with detergent soap. It burned.

Mami called out again, "*Raquel, muchacha,* come on." "*Ya voy, Mami,*" I yelled back, "I'm in the bathroom."

I ran to my room, found new panties, put them on, put on clean long pants and a blouse with sleeves and ran toward the door. When I reached the door, I turned and ran back to the bathroom, took out the ripped panties and stuffed them in my pocket, then raced down the hallway stairs. I rummaged through my book bag, so I wouldn't have to look into *Mami's* piercing eyes.

"How many times have I told you not to leave your things on the stoop, Raquel?"

"Sorry, *Mami,* I had to go to the bathroom real bad." "*Mija,* those clothes are too nice for the beach. Won't you be hot? Never mind, we're late already, *vamonos.* "

Whew, I thought.

We began our parade down the block to the Longwood Avenue train station, each one of us, *Mami,* Venus, *Madrina,* her daughters *Maricarmen,* Isabel, the twins Yvonne and Elena, and even Frankie reluctantly trailing behind the others. Everyone carried something—a shopping bag, towels, blankets, the cooler, beach chairs for *Madrina* and *Mami.* I walked behind Frankie sneering at him with venom and hate in my eyes. I hated him and I hated his friend.

We got onto the train that took us to the last stop, Pelham Parkway. Once inside, we traveled from one car to the next until we hit the last car. I sat by myself, in one of the two-seated corners. They usually left me alone when I was reading, so I hid behind my book. My behind still burned, but I couldn't stand because the train was empty and *Mami* might wonder so I sat with my nose in my book bit back my tears and ignored the pain.

The ride to Pelham Parkway took forever. This ride was usually a big thrill for me now, I was no longer afraid of *el monstro.* I'd stand and sway to the movement of the train as it raced down the dark tunnel toward somewhere. Suddenly, it would burst out into a lighted station, the signs whizzing by, Third Avenue, Brook Avenue, 145th Street, and so on. We traveled in the late morning, after rush hour, when the train wasn't as crowded so we could dance to the *conga drum* jam sessions that began on the subway and continued on the beach. Young Mongo Santamaria wannabes thumping away while we clapped along, shimmying and shaking our hips. Some of the young *salseras* used the train pole as a make-believe dancing partner, moving to and from it in their rhythmic mambo performances. Just before the train pulled out from the tunnel at Prospect Avenue, I'd jump to the window to get the best view. It was exciting to see the hole of light in the distance become bigger and bigger, as you raced toward it, till suddenly we'd rush through it and come out of the pitch black tunnel over a city landscape of buildings, traffic and sky. Today though, I could care less. I'd have given anything to be in my room hiding underneath the covers.

Finally, we reached the last stop. It was another half-hour walk to the beach. As everyone surrounded *los congeros,* I crept along slowly, trying to minimize the pain in my ass, willing back my tears and the urge to scream and punch somebody.

I began talking to God in my head, "How could you let this happen?" Instead of being angry with the boy who raped me, I was angry with God for letting this happen to me. I was angry with myself for not being strong enough to fight him off. I, the first soprano who could belt out a song loud enough for the neighbors across the street to hear, or bellow like *Mami* calling me home from outdoors, had, in a moment of crisis when it was most important, lost my voice.

God, I asked, *what sin had I committed to have this happen to me?* Perhaps that's what the nuns meant when they said you were born with sin, which is why you had to be baptized right away. Maybe it's because I wasn't baptized till I was seven years old? I guess by that time, I must have racked up a great deal of venial sins that had blown up into one huge mortal sin. Why did *Mami* and *Abuela* wait so long to baptize me anyway? Why had God punished me this way? I cooked for my mother, I cleaned house, washed my baby sister's diapers, did the dishes, the laundry and even kept Venus's side of our bedroom clean. I always did my homework, got good grades and was never late to school. I hadn't even played hooky yet, though I had been thinking about it. Could that be it? Was thinking about playing hooky bad enough to merit such a punishment? Maybe it's because I resented doing all that housework. Still, I did it. Didn't that count for anything? Or maybe it was because I was nasty to my biological father, Angel, on our weekly Sunday-morning-after-church-fifteen-minute visits. *Por que! Why, why, why?*

When something like this happens to a young girl in our neighborhood, people would immediately say, "She must have asked for it. I saw her, talking with that *muchacho.* This is what she gets for talking with boys." It was always the girls' fault. No one ever said anything about the boy. I was ashamed and scared, absolutely sure that if anyone found out, I'd be thrown out of the family, rejected forever. Last year, when my friend *Taina,* who lived in the building next door, got pregnant, her father beat her up, then threw her out of the house. I watched from my bedroom window as she sat in front of the basement doorway all night long, crying and hugging herself. I cried too. I brought her down a coke and a big bag of Wise potato chips and held her tight while she ate and shivered and cried. Well, that wasn't going to happen to me, no way. I was the only one who knew what happened and that's the way I was going to keep it. I resolved never to tell anyone about it, ever.

The more I secretly yelled my questions at God, the more I lagged behind. By now you couldn't tell if I was on my own or with *Mami* and the crowd, except when she periodically yelled, "Hurry up, Raquel." I'd run to catch up a little, just enough not to get yelled at anymore. I was sick of that too.

Once we arrived at the beach, the ritual of changing into our bathing suits began. *Mami* and *Madrina* would put

up a big towel and one by one we'd crawl inside, shed our
clothes and put on our bathing suits. We all thought it was
fun to get undressed and then slip into our bathing suits
out in the open. We'd giggle and jump up and down with
excitement, but I couldn't do it this time. "I have to go to
the bathroom," I said, rushing off quickly before *Mami* could
stop me. When I arrived at the public baths, I found a stall,
went in and threw up again. When I pulled up my pants I
noticed I had black and blue marks on my legs, so I just
pulled them back on. I found the ripped panties I'd stuffed
in my pocket and shoved them down to the bottom of the
garbage can, along with my bathing suit. I washed my arms
up to my elbows, partly rolled up my long sleeves, then put
cold water on my face.

When I returned to our blanket *Madrina* asked if I
wanted *un sandwiche*. For the first time in my life, the thought
of food made me sick. I wanted to vomit again, but I
swallowed hard, held it back and said, "*No, gracias, Madrina.*"
They all and stared at me in amazement. I never turned
down food. "After I swim," I yelled, running toward the
ocean. I dunked myself in the water, clothes and all. Instead
of playing with my sister and *MariCarmen* and *Isabel*, I sat
quietly wading in the ice-cold water, wishing the ocean would
swallow me up. That wasn't likely, because we were never
allowed to go any deeper than up to our knees. After a while
my *culito* was numb from the ice cold water. Usually I'd
quickly dunk in the water to cool off, then lie in the sun and
stare at the ocean daydreaming or play in the sand, but,
today was different. I stayed in that freezing Atlantic Ocean
for hours until I looked pruny, my lips were purple and my
teeth chattered rapidly. Finally, *Mami* came over and insisted
I come out, actually she tiptoed in, dragged me out and
wrapped me up in a towel. "What's wrong with you today,
Mija?" I just shrugged my shoulders, lay down on the blanket,
wrapped my towel around me and opened my book. After a
while I fell asleep.

That was the second time that day I awoke to the sound
of *Mami*'s voice, "*Raquel, Raquel, Mija*, wake up. It's time to
go." Everything was packed except the blanket I slept on.
Mami rubbed my forehead, looking affectionately into my
eyes. "*Como estas nena*, does your tummy still hurt?"

"How did you know my tummy hurt, *Mami*?"

"*Nena*, when you don't eat, something's got to be wrong.
What else could it be?"

"I'm better now *Mami*, really."

As we walked back to the train station, I realized that so
far I had managed to fool everyone. Good, my plan was
working. I just had to put it out of my mind and keep it that
way forever.

11

FORGETTING

For the rest of the summer I tried to be as normal as I could. No one seemed to notice that I no longer sat alone on the stoop to read or play jacks, nor did they notice that that I didn't sing or play my records anymore. Instead, I took to sitting on the front windowsill or I'd only sit on the stoop with *Doña Provi* during her daily afternoon break. Each day at around 3:30 in the afternoon she'd bring out her chair and knitting bag and sit and watch as we played jump rope or pick-up sticks. She watched us happily and hardly ever worked on her knitting. I would sit really close to her, quietly reading my book. The minute she left, I'd fly upstairs and go back to my windowsill. Over time, I willed my mind not to think of that day. I erased it.

By mid-November of 1958 I had settled into my fall routine of going to school, doing my homework and cleaning chores, and of course, reading. I'd also taken to sitting on my bed in the dark and rocking till I fell asleep. I called it my quiet time and everyone just assumed I was going through a phase and being a little moody.

Two nights a week, *Mami* and I took the Third Avenue L then got off at Jackson Avenue and walked the rest of the way to *Papito*'s store. *Casa Castaño* was flourishing now and *Papito* had a partner, *Don Pepe Dalmau, Tia Argelia's* husband. He did all the repairs and refurbishing of appliances, while Papito worked on the furniture and moving. It was filled with old rocking chairs, tables, lamps and refrigerators, and washing machines and junk that *Papito* and *Pepe* would rescue and then carefully restore. Together they'd replace nuts and bolts and wires, then clean, strip, polish and paint things until they looked almost new. Then they'd sell them. That's how we got our first washing machine, the kind with the roller that wrings the clothes dry. When we visited the store, I would follow *Papito* around, calling myself his assistant and asking questions, while the real assistant, my mother, wrote letters, worked on the ledgers and paid the bills. Watching *Papito*, I learned to fix things, paint, put up wallpaper and strip and refinish old furniture.

Venus never really liked the store. "It's too messy," she'd say. She preferred to stay with *MariCarmen* and *Isabel* playing. After the work was done, the three of us would drive home in *Papito*'s truck. I'd sit in the middle and keep my hand on the transmission stick so that each time *Papito* had to move it, he'd touch my hand, making me feel like I was helping him drive.

One evening, as *Mami* and I jaywalked toward the store in the middle of the street under the Jackson Avenue station, people started yelling. We looked around to see where the ruckus was coming from and saw a man running very fast in our direction. Lot's of people stopped to watch what was going on, "*Mira, mira,*" they'd say, "look!" The man kept racing toward us and turning to look behind him. Two cops were chasing him. He was going so fast, he didn't see the

big truck coming toward him. Suddenly, there was a huge
screeching sound, then a thump, and people began yelling.
"*Ay Diós mio*, help, police, help."

The truck threw him toward us and he landed right at
our feet, his legs twisted awkwardly and his arms spread out
as if they'd come out of the sockets. A crowd formed and
pushed *Mami* and me nearer to him. I took off my glasses,
squinted closely at him and gasped before *Mami* could turn
my head away. It was he, the boy who broke my *culito*. "Serves
him right," I blurted out! *Mami* slapped me.

"*Muchacha*, what are you saying, the man's just been
killed!" She crossed herself quickly.

"Yes," I said, "*esta muerto.*"

I didn't cry, I didn't say I was sorry, and I didn't make the
sign of the cross. I thought to myself angrily looking up at
the sky, *he'd better be going to hell, God.*

There he was sprawled out at my feet, dead. Secretly I
was glad, but it didn't make feel any better. I only knew I was
right never to have told anyone about what he did to me.
Now I no longer had to be afraid that he'd come back to
hurt me. I didn't forgive him and I didn't forgive God. I just
shoved the memory of both terrible experiences back into
the deepest recesses of my mind for good.

Over time, the memory and pain of the rape receded,
but the legacy of the violation haunted me in other ways.
Now I was labeled "square" because I "wouldn't put out" as
they said in those days. The last thing I wanted was for some
boy to start pawing all over my body. If a guy even got too
close to me I'd cringe and step back. I'd insult them or walk
away. Almost all the girls I knew who "put out" got pregnant,
but I was determined. That wasn't going to happen to me! I
wasn't going to get stuck in the *barrio*. It's not that I was
ashamed of being from the *barrio*, I just didn't want to get
stuck there forever. I had plans. I was going to college. I was
going to be a famous singer, though since that dreadful day,
I didn't do much singing. I wanted to see Spain, Europe

and all of Latin America. I was going to do it all. I was going somewhere beyond this filthy, dangerous neighborhood full of gangs, violence, strange men, drugs and garbage. I need not think about this anymore, *punto!*

12

WEST SIDE STORY, TAKE TWO

One of the few places *Mami* let me hang out at after school was at the PAL—Police Athletic League— right across the street from our building on 156th Street. After school I'd usually go and play ping pong and practice for my track meets with my favorite coach, Sonny Rodriguez. He was cute, short and muscular with sandy blond hair. And, he was Puerto Rican. He ran all the sports events at the PAL, and I had a crush on him because he was very soft-spoken and courteous. I'd already won two medals in the one-hundred-yard dash in the annual PAL competition, thanks to Sonny's training.

The other coach I really liked was Freddie Orange, the "art director" at the center. Freddie was wonderfully eccentric, funny and encouraging. He was always laughing and joyful, and I loved being around him. He seemed so worldly and sophisticated. He was the only man I knew who wore bright colors and the tightest jeans I'd ever seen.

In April of 1961, we began the preparations for the annual PAL summer musical activity and this year Freddie Orange had decided that we would perform a musical. "We're going to do *West Side Story*," Freddie said, fluttering his arms excitedly. "We'll take it to all the centers in the city." I don't know how he thought we were going to pull that off, but I was game. I had seen the movie a dozen times because Rita Moreno was in it, and I loved her and the film. It was great to see a *Puertorriqueña* on the big screen who could do it all—sing, dance, act, and was excellent. As far as I was concerned, she was as good as anyone else on that stage and better than most, especially Natalie Wood. I liked Natalie as an actress, she was great in *Splendor in the Grass*, but a Puerto Rican she wasn't. Years later I'd have a different perspective about this movie. There are things I liked about it: the music, the songs, the costumes, the choreography and the dancing. And there are things I didn't like, like Natalie Wood playing a Puerto Rican and the stereotypical, almost comical, portrayal of gangs. But at the time, almost every Puerto Rican or Hispanic I knew wanted to see that film and loved it because Rita Moreno was in it and was absolutely fabulous, and, she was one us!

Freddie had decided that it was going to be an open-audition session, meaning that teens from all the PAL centers in the other boroughs across New York City, Brooklyn, Queens, Manhattan and Staten Island, could participate. It would be like going on tour with a play.

For two weeks I practiced my singing and dancing every day. On the day of the audition, I wore the brand new black pedal pushers I had made with a white blouse and tied a bright red scarf around my neck to complement my green silk purse heirloom from *Titi Maria*. I packed my dance leotards and rehearsal shoes, just in case. I had taken ballet classes for about eight years now so I could dance as well as sing. But singing was my favorite. Everyone said it was my natural, God-given talent. I had practiced every night and I was prepared to put my heart into this audition and get the part.

I got there early to help Freddie set up the registration table. There were lots of new faces, mostly boys, and as I looked around I saw him—Alfonso—for the first time. He was tall and slender; he oozed intelligence and wore glasses, like me. For a guy, he had the most beautiful hands with long, tapered fingers that looked manicured like a piano player's, only they weren't. His gaze was intense. When he looked straight into my eyes, for the first time in my life my heart skipped a beat, butterflies began dancing in my stomach and my fingers trembled. *Be cool*, I said to myself, *don't be too forward, boys don't like that.* So I looked down at my hands instead of into his gaze and thought to myself, *Wow, this is the one!* How does one know that someone you've just seen across the room is suddenly and so clearly the one? Is this what they call chemistry or kismet? In the distance I heard my name called. It was my turn to audition. Up until then I was so sure of myself, but now I became nervous. My hands were clammy and the butterflies in my stomach were dancing up a storm, was it him or the audition?

I took a deep breath, walked to the center of the room, focused my eyes on Freddie Orange and belted out the best "I Feel Pretty" I could muster, when what I felt was nervous and silly and awkward. But I pulled it off, and when it was over, he smoothly walked across the room and congratulated me. His name was Alfonso, he lived on 125th Street in East Harlem, and he was Puerto Rican too.

"What are you doing way over here?" I asked.

"I came for the auditions," he said, "and I'm ever so glad I did."

That really did a number on my butterflies. His voice was deep and his words clear and articulate. I prayed he'd get the part of Tony and hoped he'd offer to walk me home.

Half my prayer was answered. He asked if he could walk me home and I said yes before he finished the sentence. The other half would have to wait till next week, when Freddie would announce who he chose for the parts.

Since I only lived across the street from the PAL, I guided us in the opposite direction. We walked two blocks toward my old elementary school, then down to Southern Boulevard, then over to Longwood Avenue and finally up to Beck Street stretching it from one block to six blocks. At every corner we'd stop for a while and continue talking till we finally reached my front entrance.

"Must you go in yet?"

Oh, that voice, how it made my butterflies do triple pirouettes.

"Yeah, I'd better, I'm already late and *Mami* will be angry. Pretty soon she'll come out the door screaming my name."

We stood inside between the main entrance and the second door and just looked at each other. He took my hand and I swear I was gonna faint. The long slow walk toward home in the opposite direction was to become one of our rituals. Twice a week Alfonso came to our PAL, we'd rehearse the play, and then he'd walk me home. Another one of our rituals was our Sunday visits. After church I'd take the train to his home and walk from Lexington Avenue train stop to the projects on 125th Street and First Avenue. Sometimes we'd make a picnic and walk over the Triboro Bridge to Randall's Island and hang out. Alfonso and I, his best friend Manny and his girlfriend Sophia, Alfonso's younger sister, Miriam, with her boyfriend Paul, and sometimes Freddie Orange would hang out with us too. Afterwards we'd return to his home and have Sunday dinner with the family. Al's mother was a great cook, like my *Abuela,* and she made delicious typical Puerto Rican food—rice with red beans and chicken, or steak smothered in onions with crispy fried *tostones (plantains).* She was a genius in the kitchen and we all gobbled it up: Al and I, his two sisters Sandy the youngest, and Miriam, and Paul, who was attached to Miriam by an invisible string.

Alfonso's parents were a perfect example of the racially mixed culture Puerto Ricans come from, as was my family. Doña Berta was very fair with carrot red curly hair and large brown eyes. And Don Alfonso was the color of rich dark roast coffee, with shiny jet-black wavy hair, and when he smiled, his white teeth sparkled just like his happy eyes. Don Alfonso was always cool and calm, while Dona Berta hovered over her brood with nervousness and joy.

After about six months of seeing Alfonso at the PAL during rehearsals (we got the parts of Tony and Maria) or at his house after church, instead of staying for catechism class or hanging out at Hunts Point with my girlfriends, I decided to introduce him to my parents. I told my mother I'd met a nice guy and I wanted him to come over for dinner. When I told her I'd met him at the PAL, her response was "He can't possibly be nice if he came from there."

"Well, I go there," I retorted.

She looked at me from the corner of her eye, fighting a smile that really wanted to take over with that you-got-me that-time look. That evening, the topic of my new boyfriend was discussed around the dinner table. I was so scared to bring it up I couldn't eat, but I had promised Alfonso that I'd ask. Besides, I was tired of sneaking around all the time. The response was typical.

"You're too young to have a *novio*, you have to concentrate on school, *Señorita*," said *Mami* and *Abuela* simultaneously. They always did that, one in English the other in Spanish.

"Mi amor, don't you think it's better to meet *el novio* than to have her sneaking around in dark hallways to be with him?" said *Papito* in his soft, persuasive voice.

So after a good hour of everyone around the table gleefully teasing me, it was agreed I could invite him over for dinner the next Saturday. *Whew, that was torture!*

Of course, Venus continued teasing relentlessly for the rest of the week. Every time she opened her mouth, she'd have some snide remark to make.

"So, tell me, since you're both four-eyed, do you take your thick pointy eyeglass off or does he just peck you on the cheek? Is he a smarty-pants intellectual like you—always reading books?"

All day long she repeated, "Na na na na na, Raquel's got a boyfriend, na na na na na, he dances ballet and wears glasses. Hey, he likes dancing . . . does that mean he's a *mariconcito?*"

On and on she'd nag till I thought I'd go crazy. She was pretty slick, though she never said things like this in front of the adults.

Finally, Saturday was here. I got up early, washed and put my hair in rollers, and began my house cleaning duties. After I finished the main part of the apartment, which took all morning, I was working on our bedroom, which I always do last. Venus was following me around the entire day being a pain in the butt.

"Oops, you missed a little speck of dust here, dearie. Oh by the way, I think you should keep your rollers on when he comes. What are you gonna wear with them, your pedal pushers or a skirt? Remember what *Los Abuelo*s say—keep your eyes open and your legs crossed."

She just wouldn't let up. I kept thinking, I'm going to strangle her! In spite of Venus's constant teasing, I finished all my chores and was now ready to shower. When I got to the bathroom, she wouldn't let me in. I went back to our room, sat on my bed and crossed my legs tight because I had to pee so badly. It was about a half-hour before she came out and my groin was beginning to ache.

"You'd better hurry up and take your shower, dearie, four-eyes will be here soon and you're all smelly and sweaty."

As I got up to go the bathroom, it was like my bladder burst and I peed on myself. Venus didn't wait a minute . . .

"Hah, wait till I tell your four-eyed sweetie about this."

That was it, the next thing I knew I had her by the neck with half of her body out of the window. I kept holding her tighter and tighter as she pulled at my hair and gasped for air. In the distance I heard a soft voice repeating my name.

"Raquel, Raquel, Raquelita?"

I looked up and saw that it was our tenant Marta. I thought everyone was out. I looked down and saw my hands around Venus's neck. I blinked many times. I felt as if I'd left my body and then returned. I was hot and had chills, then suddenly my head ached, as if I'd just woken up from a nightmare, and discovered I'd snapped and lost control of myself. When I realized what I was doing it freaked me out. My skin and bones went cold when I realized that I could be rattled that way and that I could lose control, that I could be violent. I started crying and begging her to forgive me then I ran to the bathroom, slammed the door and sat on the bowl shivering. I had almost killed my sister. It's true Venus drove me nuts, but I was the older sister, I should know better, right? In spite of the fact that she was such a pain, I did love her, she was my little sister. It's funny how you can love someone who's mean or teases you and makes you angry. I often pondered this same question about Mami, whom I both adored and became infuriated by. Yet, in time I'd forgive her. I'd get angry with Venus too because she was such a drag sometimes, yet deep down I felt a special bond with her that would overtake my anger. And so, like *Mami* and *Papito,* I spoiled her by not telling them about all her mischievous pranks. I helped create the monster.

I took a long hot shower to calm down. When I returned to our bedroom, Venus was sitting on the edge of her bed very still and quiet. I'd never seen her like that before. When my parents came, I told them what had happened. It scared me so much I had to. Yet, they seemed not as worried as I was, in fact *Mami* turned to Venus and said,

"Well, my dear, I guess you won't be picking on your big sister anymore, will you?"

Venus never teased me that way again. Never! But, the thought that I could lose control so completely frightened me then, and haunts me still. I resolved to learn to be patient with her and with everyone else.

That evening during Al's first visit, Venus behaved beautifully. She sat next to him and was surprisingly as quiet as a mouse. *Abuela* made the most delicious dinner, and *Alfonso* kept comparing her cooking to his mother's. *Papito* liked *Alfonso* a lot because he looked like a serious young man and they talked about history. *Mami* thought he had big mysterious eyes (that means bedroom eyes in her book) and was very smart—that's very important to *Mami*. *Abuela* thought he was courteous. *Abuelo* didn't say a word; he'd probably tell *Abuela* what he thought later on. I walked *Alfonso* downstairs to the main entrance. As he left, he pressed a ring on my finger. When I returned I announced that we were going steady.

What my family didn't know is that Alfonso and I had already decided we were soul mates and in love. We were going to get married right after graduating high school and go to college together. But, they didn't need to know that just yet!

13

CHANGES, CHANGES AND MORE CHANGES!

As Christmas and New Year's approached in 1961, no one seemed to be into the holiday spirit. This was surprising because we loved this time of year. It seemed life was changing all around me, and I didn't like it. Everyone was moving. It began with *Titi María* who, after taking me on my first trip to her beloved homeland, decided to live out the rest of her days in Puerto Rico. Now *Los Abuelos* had decided to move to Queens to be closer to *Abuelita*'s job so she wouldn't have to get up at 3 a.m. to get to work by 5 a.m. I knew I should have been glad for her and for *Abuelo* since he always got up at that time to walk her to the train station, but I would miss them terribly, so I couldn't be totally happy about it. I know it's selfish, but I'd grown up with *Los Abuelo*s: First, I had lived with them in their basement apartment then they lived with us, and I liked it that way.

Even Sylvia had met her Mister Right! At first I was happy because it meant I'd get my own room and not have to share one with my messy sister, but *Papito* said he'd have to take in two new tenants to make ends meet, so there went that dream. First, I lose *Titi María,* now *Abuelo* and *Abuelita,* I don't get my own room, and I have to clean up after two new people I didn't even know.

And just in case that weren't enough, *Mami* and *Papito* were thinking of going modern in style, so now the living room furniture was to change as well. They decided to give the plush forest green sectional sofa set with the gray tassel trimming to *Abuela* and *Abuelo* and buy a new Danish style sofa. *Ugh,* the shape was so square and the cushions were so thin, it wasn't comfortable for sitting still and reading, much less rocking.

"Why couldn't *Papito* find something nice for *Abuelo* and *Abuela* in his second-hand store? That way we could keep our comfy plush sectionals that I loved to rock on."

"Precisely," said *Mami,* "that's why we're getting the modern sofa, *Mijita,* so you can't rock on it and ruin the cushions. Besides it's time for a new style, a more modern look. What I really wish is that we could move out of this rotten neighborhood to Babylon, Long Island or to Connecticut, where many of our friends have already gone. It's clear that's not going to happen for a while, so for now, new furniture will have to suffice, even if I'm not that crazy about it. Anyway, changing the subject, it's time for you to go to church, Raquel, and then see your father Angel, and don't forget the envelope, please."

As I walked to church, I thought to myself, I'm going to make a change as well, a big change, something I've thought about for a long time. I'm sick and tired of these forced— Sunday visits with my biological father, *Papi Angel,* and what I hated the most was having to ask for that dumb envelope with the weekly stipend. I was tired of being trapped between *Mami* and *Papi Angel's* money battles. If *Mami* wants money, let her come here every Sunday and ask for it. For years now, every Sunday after church I had to meet him on the corner for our weekly visit. He'd shrug his shoulders, pat me on the head and stare at me. For a grown-up he was awfully tongue-tied. After five minutes, I would ask for the envelope and say goodbye. Well, *no mas*. I've had it. This time I was making a change.

"*Hola,*" I said as I approached him, looking at his auburn reddish curly hair. Just my luck, it was the one trait that connected me to him. It was the same color as mine, but that was it, that's the only physical trait we had in common, thank goodness. My older brother Junior was the one who looked almost exactly like him and still does—with fair skin, rosy cheeks, light auburn curly hair, same height, five feet five inches, and same chunky body type. My brother Victor is taller, with reddish-brown skin, like *Abuelo*, and a kinky "Afro" hairstyle. I'm the *mulatica*, with reddish curly hair, yellowish skin and hazel-green eyes. We were a perfect example of a typical Puerto Rican family, made up of all these different skin and eye color combinations, a mixture of our rich ancestry of Taino Indians, Africans and Spaniards busting out all over.

"Hola," Papi Angel replied, shrugging his shoulders and patting me on the head.

"How is *la escuela?*" he asked.

"School's OK," I said, shrugging my shoulders too, "but I don't want to talk about that. I want to ask you a question."

He shrugged his shoulders again.

"Why do we meet on the street corner and not at your home or my home? *¿Por que?* How come you never take me to the park or the zoo, or anywhere, not even to your house so I can see my *hermanos*, Angel Jr. and Victor?"

Again, he shrugged his shoulders, "That's just the way it is, *Nena*."

So I also shrugged my shoulders and replied, "Well, not any more! I'm not coming here to meet you and pick up the envelope any more. From now on if you want to see me, you can come to my house and pick me up and give the check to *Mami* yourself or mail it. *Punto!*"

I pivoted sharply and walked off. I could feel my cheeks burning and my auburn curls bouncing on my shoulders as I fought the urge to look back. He didn't even call after me. So I had to turn and look. He was still there, standing with a stunned look on his face, his hands in his pockets and his shoulders shrugged so tight he looked like he didn't have a neck.

When I arrived home, the modern Scandinavian furniture had already replaced the old family sectionals. The living room looked bigger, yet empty and cold, and the sofa looked like it would break if more than two people sat on it. Sylvia, never able to keep quiet, commented, "*Hay que nice,*" she smiled, though not too convincingly. *Abuela* tried to console me saying, "Don't worry, *Raquelita,* you can sit on your favorite sofa and rock *todo lo que quieras*—all you want— when you spend the weekends with us."

I smiled at *Abuela* and went to my room, hoping *Mami* was so distracted with her new furniture that she'd forgotten about the check, but before I'd gotten halfway down the hallway she yelled out, "*Raquel,* where's the envelope?" I kept on walking as if I hadn't heard her, but as I turned, there she was right behind me in the doorway. I defiantly blurted out a slew of questions before she could ask for the envelope again.

"Why must I always meet him on the street corner? Why can't he come here? Why don't my brothers visit me, why don't we visit each other? Why?"

"Because, my dear, that's just the way it has to be. What is this all about, anyway? And answer my question, young lady, where is the check?" *Mami* yelled.

"I forgot it," slapping my hands at my side in frustration. "Why don't you ask him to bring it here next week?" I was pushing my luck and I knew it, but I didn't care.

"Forgot it," *Mami* yelled. "I specifically reminded you before you left. You're punished, young lady, no PAL and no dates with Alfonso for the rest of the week."

"No dates, come on, *Mami,* that's not fair, I just forgot." I was really asking for it now.

"Too bad, that'll teach you not to forget anymore."

Mami stormed down the hall, stomping all the way to her bedroom. I heard her dialing the phone. *Uh oh!*

The next day I got my wish, *Papi Angel* came to the house. We were all lined up at attention in front of Mami. "Well, at least I got him to come here," I muttered to *Papito,* who frowned at me. *Mami* began badgering *Papi Angel* to tell her what happened and he kept shrugging his shoulders. Then he looked at me pleadingly; I guess he was afraid of *Mami* too. Good! I asked *Papito* to help me, but he said "*No puedo,* I can't interfere."

"That's just great; I'm trapped between *Mami* and my biological father, and abandoned by my *Papito.*"

"Don't be sarcastic, young lady," *Mami* snapped.

So I started repeating all my questions again, loudly.

"Well, you didn't answer my questions about why you don't come here to pick me up and why we never go anywhere. Why you just pat me on the head, ask about school and give me an envelope, week after week. Do you call that a visit?"

Papi Angel looked at *Mami,* shrugged his shoulders and said, "I've got a right to see my daughter, don't I?"

"So," I said, "what about my brothers, I have a right to see them, don't I? Besides, you're not my father, *Papito* is. You're just the man who kicked *Mami* in the belly so I'd come out distorted, but I'm not distorted, so there."

Mami and *Angel* and *Papito* looked stiff as mummies. I stunned them into silence. Good!

"Well, I've decided I don't want to do it that way anymore, *punto!*"

I stormed out fighting the tears and headed straight for the stoop where I sat crying and muttering next to Venus and Isabel who were playing jacks.

"I'm just not doing it that way anymore, and that's that, I'll run away from home first."

Venus retorted in her whiny know-it-all voice. "Well, that's a stupid idea; you have no money and no place to go. And besides, you don't even know how to ride the train, dummy?"

Sometimes that sister of mine came out with the most sensible comments. It was rare, but when she did, it was always at the wrong time and it pissed me off even more!

Suddenly, I saw *Papi Angel* racing out of the building without so much as a word or a gesture to me.

Mami yelled down to us from the window, "*Raquel,* you come up here this instant, young lady." "Venus, you stay right there and don't move an inch till I call for you, understand!"

I went upstairs and sat on one of the uncomfortable Scandinavian chairs that go with the new sofa, looked downward, pursed my lips and crossed my arms over my chest. I always did this when I was going to be lectured.

"*Mijita,*" *Papito* said, "you shouldn't say things like that in anger."

"Well, it's true! Besides, he never takes me anywhere, he hardly even talks to me or plays with me like you do. He's not my Papi, you are."

Mami said, "*Mijita,* I know it's difficult, but he is your natural father and you just can't say things like that and walk off, young lady. Look, we'll make a change for a while and see how it goes. We'll stop your weekly visits to see *Papi Angel* until he can get permission to come here to visit with you."

"Get permission? From whom does he have to get permission, he's a grown up?"

"Well, from his wife, Nina. She doesn't want him to come here. From now on Angel will send the weekly stipend in the mail or maybe with your brothers."

"My brothers, you mean they can come and visit?"

"Yes, *Raquel,* they'll visit once a month. OK?"

"Oh wow, that's great."

See, I thought to myself, it worked. Now I've made a change around here, and a good one at that. As they looked around the living room, *Mami* hugged me and frowned.

"*Sabes, Raquel,* maybe you're right about the furniture too. I should have left the money in the bank to save up for our move to Long Island. Oh well, *Cest la vie.*"

That was one of *Mami*'s favorite sayings. Mine was, "I can't think about that today, I'll think about it tomorrow," just like Scarlet O'Hara always said in the book *Gone With the Wind.* I was a grown-up, though, before I really understood what *cest la vie* meant.

Suddenly, Sylvia entered loudly, as usual, waving her hands and saying "*Me comprometi, mira.*" Gleefully, she kept repeating, "I'm engaged, look," as she wiggled her left hand showing us her diamond ring. She was engaged, at last! The man she was engaged to, whose name she never mentioned, owned a house.

"*Ah, y tiene una casa bella.* And guess where that beautiful house is? *Pues,* on Long Island in Babylon to be exact! So we'll be close when you move there," she stated emphatically, as she walked off toward her room, shaking her hips and staring at her ring.

"*Mami,* are you sure you want to move to Babylon? Maybe we should move in the opposite direction, like to Connecticut or next to *Titi Delis* in New Jersey."

"Or maybe California," *Mami* replied, "that's real far away?"

Papito, Mami and I laughed so hard my stomach hurt. Then *Abuelo* entered, dragging a huge Christmas tree. As we began opening the boxes and decorating the tree, which had been placed in front of our tropical landscape mural, *Abuelita* brought out her delicious home-made Puerto Rican Eggnog. Mmmm, *coquito.* She always made two kinds, one with rum for the adults and one without rum for Venus and me.

"It's about time we started getting into the Christmas spirit around here," I said, "I was getting worried."

As it turned out, the Christmas of 1962 was our last at the apartment on Beck Street, and is marked by a wonderful portrait-like photo of the four of us, seated in front of the lush Florida Everglades mural. *Papito* looked distinguished with his hair slicked back, wearing a smoking jacket, his wing-tipped black and white shoes, and sporting a pipe. *Mami* sat proudly beside him wearing her sexy black sweetheart shaped low cut dress with a shawl wrapped around her shoulders. Venus and I are wearing our ice blue dresses with the mink collars and muffs, and our collie Sabu, sits majestically beside us underneath the Christmas tree.

As we took that picture, I remember thinking that though it was often annoying living with so many people in one apartment, it was also wonderful laughing, and eating and talking together around the dinner table. That dreaded feeling in the pit of my stomach returned as I reviewed the many changes that had taken place over the last year and sensed there were more to come. Our extended family was shrinking. *Titi María* was in Puerto Rico, my grandparents were moving out and Sylvia was getting married. We were drifting away from each other like autumn leaves scattered hither and yon, further and further away from their mother tree trunk. I felt sad, for deep down in my gut I knew my family would never be the same again.

14

WESTWARD BOUND

A week after that lovely portrait was taken, on the eve of the arrival of 1963, yet another change took place. It was the first year we didn't have our annual New Year's Eve party. Deep inside, I felt a sense of misgiving that things were going to be different that year, but my premonitions paled in comparison to how drastic that difference would be.

All around me things continued to change. First, there were all the people who had moved. Next, the neighborhood had gone from being unsafe to being dangerous and no fun at all. As the neighborhood became more menacing, *Mami* and *Papito* became stricter about where we went, what time of day it was, for how long, and with whom we played. Until now, at least our block and building had been a safe haven sort of, but not anymore, for it too had become really perilous. Drugs were now being sold in the building next door and more gang members hung around on Beck Street. We were no longer allowed to play on the stoop unless there were adults with us and *Doña Provi*, now too old to be our protector, hardly ever used *la chancleta* anymore. The South Bronx had become noisier, filthier, uglier and just plane dangerous. The worse it got, the more our friends and neighbors scrambled to get out and headed for the suburbs.

My misgivings began right after one of the most joyous experiences of my childhood, when on my first trip to Puerto Rico with *Titi María*, my loving aunt, had decided to remain there instead of returning with me to the Bronx. Even though I understood why she stayed behind, and in spite of the fact that she gave me the beautiful silk purse with the heirloom emerald stone, I was devastated by her decision. I was her favorite and she was mine. Although *Titi María* was strict, she was loving and wise and we all paid attention to her, including the grownups.

Next to go was Sylvia, who finally found her dream rich man and her big expensive house in Long Island. Though she drove me crazy and made Venus angry whenever she flirted with *Papito*, she always made sure there was laughter at the dinner table and something sweet and Cuban for dessert. In the end, we all missed her sassy, bubbly personality and her raunchy sense of humor.

It was like a fever that was spreading. Right before Christmas and shortly after Sylvia departed, *La Comadre* Carmen and Don Alfredo from Apartment 8 decided to return to Puerto Rico with their five children. They sold all their furniture and winter clothes and left so quickly there was little time for goodbyes or celebration. They wanted to experience *Las Navidades* in Puerto Rico, instead of in snowy, cold New York. So Christmas was very quiet that year at 748 Beck Street and now there would be no New Year's Eve party either.

Brenda and her parents *Doña Fela* and *Don Efraín* found their dream house in Connecticut, and Rosemarie finally went to live with her mother Ginny and her third husband, a wealthy doctor, and his children on Catalina Island,

California. She went from being an only child living with her grandmother to living with a new father and two new step sisters, as well as her own half-brother and sister. She was no longer the sole little princess. The good part of it is that she'd be living on an island in the Pacific Ocean, in a big fancy house with a pool and a tennis court and soon *Doña Provi* would join them.

Then came the final blow. When Mr. Eisen, who was very lonely after his sister died, decided to retire, he sold my favorite candy store and moved to Miami to be with his cousins. I remember watching him tie up the newspapers in stacks of twenty for the garbage man. It took two months before he emptied out that room. Boy, would I miss him, no more of my special pistachio ice cream sundaes or egg cream sodas at his soda fountain shop. It was turned into a bar and all that remained were the red Formica counter and matching stools.

My world was changing around me, and I was powerless to do anything about it. Little by little the extended family at 748 Beck Street dispersed—each to a different location. I felt as if they were slowly chipping away at my life and taking a piece of me with them. If they kept it up, there wouldn't be much left. I realize now that what was dying was our way of life and my dream to keep it all as it was, my large extended family, living in an apartment building that was itself a collective extended family. Our village. I loved our building and my large family of neighbors. I loved the easy way we ran in and out of each other's apartments, played and ate together, and knew each other's business. I cherished the way we cared for and watched over each other. I loved playing jacks and reading on my stoop. I even loved it when *Dona Provi* chased us with her *chancleta,* or when we all went to Orchard Beach with *La Comadre* and ate her delicious fried chicken with Wise potato chips and sour pickles. I relished our summer gatherings on the stoop as the sounds of dominoes were slapped emphatically on the table or scrambled as they set up for a new game, while the women sat in the background telling stories, fanning themselves and keeping a watchful eye on their brood. Sometimes, I just sat and listened, taking it all in, while other times I journeyed into my own revelry hiding behind a good book with these sounds as my backdrop. When it was unrelentingly hot and humid, I joined the rest of the kids shrieking with joy as we jumped in and out of the fire hydrant's sprinkling cool water that *Papito* opened for us.

Sometimes I would sit at my special window and just watch, taking my mental pictures, as they relaxed and enjoyed themselves. My window! I would no longer sit at my window musing. That realization made me very sad. Everything I cherished—we cherished—was changing and the joy of being together wasn't strong enough to overcome the meanness and cruel attitude that spread like a cancer throughout the streets of the South Bronx. We were all running away from a neighborhood that used to nourish us and had now become a harsh, dirty, gritty, dangerous and unfriendly place.

The unspoken rule of never hurting the elders or children was no longer honored. Now gang members disrespected the elders and coaxed youngsters into trying pot and heroin. Strangers wandered the neighborhood and hid in our hallways, making deals or injecting themselves with heroin. All bets were off, any place and anyone was fair game!

When *Papito*'s best and only Cuban friend, *Don Orestes,* and his wife, Georgina, moved to San Gabriel, California, spoiling our 1963 New Year's Eve celebration ritual, he wrote and called *Papito* two and three times a week telling him and *Mami* about the wonders of living in California. It was spacious, it was warm everyday, it was safe, it was green, and there was no snow. "You don't even need a coat or gloves or boots," he'd say, "just a light jacket or *un sweatercito.*" Over and over again *Don Orestes* coaxed *Papito. "Vente chico,* get out of there, come out here and see for yourself. You'll fall in love and never return to New York."

Now that I finally had my own room, it wasn't much fun. It was lonely throughout the house and the building. My routine after school was to do my homework, then sit rocking in my darkened bedroom listening to my Ella Fitzgerald, Barbara Streisand or Xiomara Alfaro albums. All my playmates were gone and it was too dangerous to be outside.

The final blow, the one my premonitions couldn't have imagined, came in February of 1963. I arrived home from school at 3:15 p.m. sharp as usual and noticed *Papito*'s truck parked in front of our building. Puzzled, I knew something was up because he never got home this early. As I walked in the door, I heard *Mami* and *Papito* whispering intimately, but they stopped the minute I entered the room. Venus was already home and had a mile-long smile on her face, surprising since she was usually either pouting discontentedly or making snide remarks at me. She jumped out of the chair and jeered right into my face, "Nos vamos, *Papito* said so. We're moving, in three weeks, how about them apples?"

"What?"

"Yes," *Mami* repeated, "we're leaving, in three weeks. It'll be like a vacation."

"A vacation? Where are we going? *Papito*, did you play *la bolita?*"

"No, Raquel, you know I don't play *la bolita*, that's *Abuela*'s game."

"Did *Abuela* win la bolita again?" I asked with my hands in the air.

"*Pues Mija,*" mimicked my sister in her snickering gleeful tone. "We're going to Ca-li-for-ni-a," she said emphatically. "We're driving across country on our first real vacation and we're not coming back to 748 Beck Street ever again," she said and finished her statement with an emphatic "humph!" "As soon as we get there, I'm going to take horseback riding lessons, get my license and drive to the beach on the Pacific Ocean," she rattled on and on, while I tried to clear my head and make sense of what I was hearing.

"Yes," *Papito* repeated, "*Nos mudamos, Paco* and *Georgina* convinced me, we're moving to California," he beamed with pride and joy. I'd never seen him so happy, his chest was inflated and there wasn't a wrinkle on his face. *Mami* looked just as excited, with a special twinkle in her dark brown eyes. "Yes, we're finally getting out of this rotten neighborhood, we're going right away, the sooner the better."

"But, *Mami*, I thought we were moving to Long Island when we left the Bronx," and then it hit me. She said right away! "Right away, what do you mean right away?"

"In March," Venus blurted out.

"March, are you crazy, what about school, I graduate high school in June, what about my scholarship to Hunter College, what about *Abuelo* and *Abuela*, what about *Alfonso*? You can't do this to me. I won't go. I'll stay with *Abuela* and *Abuelo*. I'm not going, I'll be eighteen soon and I'm not going and that's that," I yelled and stomped my foot then walked away.

"No, young lady, come right back here," Mother bellowed. "We are not crazy, we're just sick and tired of this ghetto, and frightened at what might happen to you and your sister. May I remind you, young lady, that you're not an adult until you're twenty-one and that is three years away. So until then, my dear, you go where we go, when we go, *punto!* You can't stay with your grandparents; they don't have the room and Grandpa will lose his welfare pension if you live with them. Now sit down and listen," she said in a softer tone. "Honey, this is the dream of a lifetime."

"Yes, but March? Why must we go then, why can't we go in late in June or better yet in July right after I graduate, just wait three more months."

"Because, Raquel, *Papito* found a job already and it begins in April." She pursed her lips and put her arms in front of her chest, her way of saying the subject was closed.

Venus was so happy it made me want to slap her. I felt sick to my stomach, and all I could do was wonder about my graduation from Walton High School, my scholarship to Hunter College and life plans with Alfonso. I finally find a decent boyfriend and now I'm moving three thousand miles away.

I immediately started planning. I had to find a way to stay, that's all there was to it, I had to. First, I called my *Titi Marina, Papi Angel's* sister, who lived in the projects at the 149th Street train stop in the Bronx, only three stops from Longwood Avenue. That's important because I needed to be able to go to the same school. The thought of living with my cousins, Julio, Terri, Ruth and Robinson was exciting. They were fun and smart, and we liked being together a lot. *Titi Marina* was my favorite aunt in the Ortiz family. My other favorite was *Tio Tin,* Gladys's father, who was *Papi Angel's* older brother. *Mami* always made sure I visited with them so I'd have some connection to the Ortiz family, especially since I almost never saw *Papi Angel.*

I asked *Titi Marina* if I could stay with them just for three months. She really wanted me to stay with them, but their apartment was very small and in one of the public housing projects. They had three very small bedrooms for six people, a living room and kitchenette. Of course, I could sleep on the sofa, but the housing projects don't allow extra persons to live in the apartments. Those stupid projects had so many rules and regulations, and they were very strict about them. They periodically inspected the apartments to make sure you hadn't wrecked the place, but also to make sure there were no extra people in the apartment, and they had guards in the front to check and see who was coming in and out of the building. They were even strict about when you could and couldn't play in the park. So, *Titi Marina* said it just wouldn't be possible. I ruled out *Tio Tin* and Gladys because they lived in Brooklyn and I needed to stay in the Bronx because of school.

When I told Alfonso about my parents' plan, he was devastated. We were supposed to be in another play together at PAL, and besides we were in love.

"We'll ask my parents," he volunteered. "You could sleep with my sisters Miriam and Sandy, or you can have my room and I'll take the sofa, or you take the sofa. I know, we'll get you a sleeping bag and you can sleep on the floor in the girls' room."

We asked his parents and they thought it would be a great idea, I was only weeks away from being eighteen and they had the space. It turns out the East Harlem projects they lived in weren't as strict, so it was decided that I'd be a cousin visiting from Puerto Rico for a few weeks and then we'd just keep extending my stay. So I went home happy as could be because I'd found a way to stay and graduate with my class from Walton High School. Then I'd get a job, and get my own little apartment until Alfonso and I could get married. I had it all worked out.

When I told *Mami*, she straightened her back, arched her right eyebrow and put her hands on her hips. "Young lady," she said as I stepped back a few paces putting some distance between us in case she was going to whack me. God, I hated when she used that tone, as if she were my teacher and not my mother. "If you think we're going to let you live with your boyfriend for three months or even for three minutes, you've got another thing coming. And, what did you say about getting your own apartment? I don't think so. You're living under my roof, wherever it may be, until you're twenty-one and married, so just get that little idea out of your head and start packing instead."

And that was that! We began purging our nine-room apartment of almost everything. We were only taking our clothes and personal belongings and our beds and the TV, because it arrived the same day as Venus was born. Everything else would be sold and we'd buy new stuff for the living room and dining room in California. Well, at least we weren't taking the stupid modern Danish furniture I hated so much.

The month of March was spent having people come over to buy stuff from us and say goodbye. We did lots of kissing and hugging and crying. Even *Papi Angel* came with my brothers Junior and Victor, only we didn't hug or kiss or cry. As usual, *Papi Angel* patted me on the head, shrugged his shoulders, but this time, he gave me a twenty-dollar bill, saying, "This is for you, *Mijita.*" He never called me that before. Then he turned away and left, pushing Junior and Victor out the door before him.

The only good thing about the impending move was that we ate out every night visiting different friends for our last farewell dinners. We visited *Titi Marina* and my four cousins, our godmother *Delis* in New Jersey, and then Gladys and her parents *Tio Tin, Titi Doris,* and her brother Raymond in Brooklyn.

We had two more days left before our drive from New York City to San Gabriel, California. Our last dinner was to be with Al's family, which I was both excited about and dreading. Al's mother, *Doña Berta,* was going to make a special Puerto Rican meal for us. Finally, I get our families together, but ironically, it's the last time we'll see each other and the last night I'll spend with *Alfonso,* till I return, that is. We had already decided to get married as soon as we could, yet now it felt as if I'd never see him again.

As we sat around the dinner table, I looked hard at everyone trying to create a permanent mental picture of this night: *Doña Berta's* lush wavy red hair, Don Alfonso's mischievous eyes, Sandy's sense of humor, and Miriam's gentle smile and soulful eyes. After a delicious dinner of *carne mechada* (roast beef) rice and beans, and avocado, lettuce and tomato salad, the adults went to the living room for their coffee. Dessert would come later, so Alfonso and I went to his room for our last private time together. Even though the door was open, we sat on his bed. The minute he held my hand I began sobbing. We made promises to write to each other every day, and call each other once a week. We left pretty late that night. I hadn't cried this much since *Titi María* stayed in Puerto Rico.

We awoke early on our final day to unmake the beds so *Papito* could take them apart and pack them into our U-Haul trailer. As it turns out, nobody bought the ugly Danish living room furniture, so we had to take it with us. *Abuela, Mami* and I did the final cleaning touches of the apartment, which had to be left "spic-n-span" clean for the landlord or he wouldn't give us back our deposit. Even Venus helped this time; she was happy to move, wasn't she? Then we loaded our luggage into the trailer and gave the keys to our landlord, Mr. Catalano, who was sad to see his favorite super leave.

Many of our friends from 748 Beck Street came by to wish us goodbye, even Sylvia showed up with her new husband, *Andres,* and, of course, *Abuelo* and *Abuela*. But I hadn't expected to see Alfonso. What a wonderful surprise, he showed up bright and early in the morning and hugged and kissed me right in front of my parents, then handed me a card asking me not to open it until we left New York State. I was so touched that he showed up that I started bawling all over again.

It was a beautiful cutout card he'd made in the shape of a girl. He wrote a special love poem on each doll, one for each month. I hugged it close to my heart. Twelve dolls, twelve months till we'd be together again. So many changes and so many people and memories left behind. The pain in my heart was deep and heavy. That anvil again, it felt just like the day I left Puerto Rico.

After an hour of hugging and kissing and making promises to stay in touch, *Papito* piled us into the Buick. He started the engine and I turned looking out of the rear window. Click, another mental picture, this time of 748 Beck Street. I saw myself on the windowsill and waved. As we drove away toward a new life in California, I recalled my first frightening trip from *Abuela*'s house to the funeral parlor, wondering what strange surprises we'd find three thousand miles from 748 Beck Street in *El Bronx*.

Again, that heavy weight of pain pressed against my chest, for I was saying goodbye to my life as I had known it, to people loved, memories shared, dreams thwarted. As we drove out of New York State, I pondered many questions . . . just like in the song Barbra Streisand sings . . ."Where am I going and what will I find?" Will we live in an apartment building or in a house? Will there be Puerto Ricans there? What will school be like? Will I graduate this year? Most important of all, will I see Alfonso again? Will he wait for me, will he still love me?

The tears just wouldn't abate. I hated my parents. Their need to protect us was destroying my life and the plans I had to marry. I was angry with them for being afraid and hated the gangs and my neighborhood for betraying us. I resented Venus's joy about the move. I even hated California, a place I hadn't seen yet. I was angry with Alfonso for not being able to fix it, for not being old enough to marry me right then and there. I was angry at my Beck Street extended family for leaving our wonderful building. At Mr. Eisen for closing down the soda shop and moving to Florida; la *Comadre Casilda* and *Don Alfredo* for moving to Puerto Rico; the Rhondas for moving to Connecticut; Sylvia for getting married, and Rosemarie and *Doña Provi,* for going to live with her mother on Catalina Island.

I hated moving. It was always traumatic. First, when I was born and we moved in with my grandparents, then when Mami married Papito and we moved into the apartment over the funeral parlor, and now this move, three thousand miles away from anything I knew and everyone I loved. Moving meant destruction and separation. It means taking everything down, changing the shape and look of your life and leaving the people and places you love behind. It changes your plans and distorts your dreams. I prayed for

Alfonso to chase the car, open the door and pull me out of it, but alas, he couldn't. As the image of my 748 Beck Street and Alfonso faded away, I swore I would never forgive my parents for taking me away from my home and my soul mate. I touched *Titi Maria's* tiny silk purse around my neck, reconnecting to that first pain of loss and her words echoed, "You know I'll always be with you, *Siempre!*"

15

HUELLAS *AND REFLECTIONS*

I've traveled a convoluted and interesting road since the day of that wrenching move from Beck Street to California. As I reflect upon those pivotal moments of my South Bronx childhood, I clearly see the *huellas* they left upon me. Imprints, indelible and haunting, pressed upon my soul.

Beginning with my tumultuous welcome into the world, the recording and archiving of these milestones in the darkest corner of my little heart took root. My father's brutal rejection! The loss of *El Piano,* and with it that special connection to my sister, Venus, and my God-given talent. Next came *Titi Maria's* surprise decision to remain in her homeland. Then my traumatic rape and the loss of my desire to sing.

The final blow was the sudden separation from my home, my neighborhood and first love, Alfonso. All that loss and pain squelched into that little bodily organ—the heart. Slowly and quietly they festered replacing my dreams and love with fear and anger.

Yet on the outside, no one, not even I, had a clue of the poisonous brew that was stewing, for I was busy participating in life and making the best of what my crossroads offered. I graduated from San Gabriel High School in California, and began working as a dental assistant and supported my family for a year until *Papito* found steady work. I knew that part-time job with Dr. Green would come in handy.

A year and a half after our move out west, *Mami* was summoned back to New York for *Abuelita* had been hospitalized and someone needed to take care of *Abuelo*. To my surprise and delight she sent me, saying she needed to watch over *Papito* and Venus.

On the flight back east, all I could think of was *Alfonso;* I couldn't wait to see him. As soon as I landed, I went straight to Metropolitan Hospital to check on *Abuela*. Her condition was stable. I then went to the apartment to see *Abuelo* and drop off my bags, then rushed to *Alfonso's* apartment. But when I arrived he wasn't there. His sister Miriam told me he'd become very despondent after I left and began cutting classes, hanging out late, and sank into a black hole of depression. Finally, accepting that we'd probably never be together again, he decided to pursue a career as a dancer and took off with his longtime friend. He traveled extensively and kept his distance from everyone. "We've lost touch with him," she said sadly. I was devastated, but I understood. Years later, when we finally saw each other, the love was there, but the pieces just didn't fit. He had a new life and a wife and I had a boyfriend. The ache in my heart was indescribable.

Once *Abuela* recouped from her surgery and returned home, I decided to stay and began working at my first job as a bilingual secretary at an international publishing firm. I attended the Fashion Institute of Technology at night and worked a few singing gigs on weekends. After a terrible experience with a sleazy potential agent, who wanted favors

I wasn't willing to give, I decided to quit singing until I could learn more about the business side of entertainment. Two weeks later, I lost my secretarial job. Now what? A new plan, of course.

After an extensive search, I accepted an administrative assistant position at the newly created Corporation for Public Broadcasting. Even though they paid less than I had been making, my gut told me there was a future here. I was right. We were building an American media institution and I became a part of that process. In my thirty-five years within public broadcasting, I worked my way up the ranks learning the business from the ground up and eventually became producer, host and writer of my own TV series, *La Plaza*, at WGBH, Boston and in two years was promoted to executive producer. After a dozen years at WGBH, I took another leap of faith and formed my own company with colleague and friend, Sharon Simon. I'm proud to say Ortiz/Simon Productions produced many good projects, including a pivotal documentary on the history of relations between Puerto Rico and the United States, a legacy to my family and heritage. I kept myself busy all the time and gave my best to the Latino community. I served on various national boards and traveled to Europe and Latin America for business and pleasure.

I had fun too, for I played as hard as I worked, surrounded by colleagues and friends who loved salsa dancing, movies, good food and travel. I expended myself in hard work that led to many accomplishments and honors, ambrosia that helped to hide the pain. Pain, that inevitably erupted.

As I reflect upon the circumstances of my childhood, I see now that my parents unwittingly made decisions that had negative consequences on my life. Their well intentioned zesl to us out of the decaying and increasingly dangerous South Bronx ghetto, three months shy of my high school graduation was, ironically, too late to protect me from being raped. Though I had squelched those memories somewhere deep down in the recesses of my psyche, just like I hid my panties deep down in the garbage can at Orchard Beach that terrible day in 1956, slowly and steadfastly the memories inched their way to the surface. Twenty-two years later, after three severed relationships and years of therapy, I worked up the courage to tell my parents about that dreadful autumn day.

I married for the first time at age twenty-seven. At last, I'd met a man who treated me like a whole person, and "not like a fine-looking chick" or "a good piece of ass," which is how guys sized you up in those days. I often wondered if being raped had left me with some special pheromone, discernible only by men that made them just see me from the neck down, breasts, hips and ass, and assume I was easy. Nothing could be further from the truth. I was locked up so good you couldn't get next to me.

Thankfully Roy was different. He thought I had a good mind, a warm personality, and yes, good looks too. What a novelty that was for me. In many ways he reminded me of Alfonso. Roy wasn't attractive but he had a brilliant mind, a great sense of humor and a gentle touch. Yes, a gentle touch, a very important quality to a woman who has been abused and violated, much more important than good looks or money or social standing. How a man approaches you the first time he enters your space is very telling. Does he intrude and grab, or approach and gently touch, and my antennae were acutely sensitive.

We met at work, dated for a year, lived together for six months, then decided to get married. The first couple of days of our honeymoon were spent strolling by the shore of Venezuela's beachside, holding hands and talking. Then we'd go back to our room and spend hours making love, with long sessions of petting before real intercourse took place. But, as the week went on Roy became more passionate, wanting me to be more experimental and playful. At first I'd giggle shyly, saying, "Are you crazy, who ever heard of such a thing?" Then

I'd try, but start gagging. After many attempts I just broke down and cried, begging for forgiveness. Throughout the week he gently kept encouraging me to be more open and playful, but whenever I tried to make him happy, I'd get sick. It was absolute torture and embarrassing to be a grown woman and behave so strangely. On the last night of our honeymoon, Roy held me in his arms until the sun rose and promised he'd never again ask me to make love to him that way. I felt an incredible sense of relief.

Sadly, our marriage didn't last long. Though I now understand there were many reasons why the relationship soured, at the time I thought it was because I couldn't make him happy in bed. In fact, it really had more to do with my parents' rejection of him, because of his age and race, than with my limitations with intimacy. Again that subject and attitude reared its ugly head in my life. However, six months after our marriage he began drinking heavily and became verbally abusive, the two things I couldn't abide and didn't suspect about him beforehand. A year later, we were separated and divorced.

Next the pendulum swung in the opposite direction and I met and dated a younger man. A couple of years into this relationship, *Armando* too wanted to explore new areas of intimacy. I loved him, so I tried over and over again, but right after making love I'd sneak into the bathroom and secretly wretch my guts out, like a woman in her first trimester, only I wasn't pregnant. For years we fought over my inability to give him what he wanted. He'd yell, I'd retort sheepishly, then he'd storm out. We'd forget for a while, but in time the subject would come up again. Finally, *Armando* just blew up at me. "I don't get it. What's the goddamn problem, I've been patient, but enough is enough," he said as he stormed out. I crawled onto the sofa and cried myself to sleep, asking myself, "Yeah, what is the problem?"

The next day, I woke up determined to fix it, to work it out. I'd see a doctor if I had to. I went to the bathroom, opened the cabinet to get my toothpaste and noticed *Armando's* toiletries were gone. I checked the closet. His side was empty. He always left in the middle of an argument, but this time, he packed all his belongings. I was devastated, five years together and—poof—he was gone. Why do they always leave without telling you? *Well, to hell with him, I'll leave too!*

I called the airlines and booked a flight to Bermuda for the next day. You could do that in those days. I packed some clothes, a bathing suit, and, God only knows why, threw in my journals. Sun and surf always made me feel better; that's why I went to Puerto Rico each year. This time, though, I chose an unknown place. The last thing I needed was the entire Puerto Rican Island asking, "*Y Armando?* Where is he, what happened?" I wanted anonymity.

At the airport I called my best friend Morgain, told her Armando and I had another fight and that I needed to get away. I gave her the details of where I was staying and told her if she didn't hear from me in two weeks to come and find me. I hung up, ran to the gate, boarded the plane, sat down, closed my eyes and slept till we landed. As we deplaned, I felt the hot blinding sun. Good, that's just what I came for. In fifteen minutes I had checked in and was ordering room service. "A bottle of dark rum, tonic water and two limes, please." I wanted numbness too. In the morning, I'd hit the beach, bathe in the warm turquoise water and bask in the hot Caribbean sun. I'd be fine in no time flat.

But the Universe had other plans. The next morning I was greeted by the sounds of a torrential downpour. The raindrops were so loud against the tin rooftop they sounded like *Tito Puente* banging away on his snare drums. For six days, morning, noon, and throughout the night, no matter when I woke up, the rain was relentless. There would be no basking in the sun for me. And, for those six days I sat holed up in my room, reading my journals and reliving memories,

Alfonso came up often. I'd read a little, muse upon the moment, then start bawling until I was exhausted and fell asleep, then I'd wake up again, have a drink and sob some more. I drowned myself in rum and tonic and tears. Each morning I'd open my eyes and peer out the window, hoping for a clear blue sky, but instead I'd hear rain thrashing against the palm trees and the metal roof. It's as if every dead person in the sky was sobbing along with me. The more I sobbed, the more it rained, and the more it poured, the more I wept. In my restless dreams I'd hear the song by Michel LeGrand, over and over again, as if I were singing it.

"Round, like a circle in a spiral, like a wheel within a wheel, never ending or beginning, like a never-spinning wheel . . ."

On the seventh day the sun glared through my window right into my eyes. My ears perked up at the sound of absolute silence. The torrent had abated. I tried to open my eyes but they were glued together. I groped my way to the bathroom, faced the mirror and pulled my right eye open to reveal a puffy face accentuated with purple bags under my eyes. It hurt to move my eyeballs so I splashed cold water on them till I got the gook out. A wasted haggard face stared back at me.

I managed to pull myself together, showered, dressed, put on my sunglasses and sun hat and headed for the dining room. After an enormous breakfast and three cups of black coffee, I ventured out. The sun was blinding and made my eyes ache again. As I headed toward the beach, I started talking to myself. *What the hell is wrong with you*, pendeja, *you're acting like a crazy woman. I'm sick of this melodrama!* I was like a boxer in training, mumbling to myself, arms flailing all over the place. The more I talked to myself, the angrier I got. I paced in this state of heated internal debate for over an hour. I was angry at everything and everyone, at the weather, at Armando, at myself, at life, at the world, at God. After walking what felt like ten miles, I reached the top of a mountain, where I found a beautiful, lonely *flamboyan* tree next to a welcoming bench. The tree's brilliant persimmon-colored flowers and branches spread out over the bench like an umbrella. There was no one else in sight. I sat down.

Mesmerized by the ocean thrashing against the shore, I began to breathe deeply. After a while, I began hearing Mother's voice calling me, *"Raquel, Raquel, Raquel."* I stood up and very cautiously approached the ledge, leaned over and spread my arms as if I was going to take off. I looked down and slowly swayed back and forth. It was thirty or forty feet to the bottom. I felt as If I'd been there before and the hair on the back of my neck stood up. Again, I heard *Mami*'s voice call to me. I contemplated flying off the edge, wondering if I'd land on the water or splat down on the hot sand. Would I break? The image of a body splashed on the ground, limbs awkwardly spread out, flashed brightly in my head. I looked down again and noticed a couple on the beach. I took off my sunglasses, squinted, and rubbed my eyes. "It's probably time for a new pair," I thought to myself. The couple was naked and in a funny position. He was pushing her from behind. With each thrust he pushed harder and faster. In my head, I heard a strange sound, a long painful moan. Suddenly my temples vibrated, my head throbbed and there was a ringing in my ears. Shit, another one of my migraines. They usually came on gradually, but this one just burst into my head like an injection.

Another chill ran up my spine and again, the image of that body strewn on the floor, legs and arms every which way, almost separated from their sockets, flashed in my head. Then I heard this strange sound come from within me. It's as if the earth had slowly begun to erupt right through my feet, up my legs, through my groin, stomach, then lungs, heart, and exploded out of my mouth in a deep moaning growl. A guttural moan that turned into a piercing howl, like the sound of a wounded mountain lion in the deep dark forest, primal and frightening. My mouth felt sticky, my saliva bitter and chalky. I felt a slimy wetness dripping all over my face, in my eyes and nose. Then came the painful and brutal sensation of my ass being ripped open. I yelled out an interminable howl—STOOOOOOOOOOOOOOP! Then I slumped down on my knees, hugged myself tightly, lay on the grass trembling and sobbing till there wasn't another drop left in me.

I awoke hearing my mother's voice calling out. *"Raquel, Raquel, wake up."* It was dark. I looked around and saw I was totally alone. I stood up, dusted my dress off and began walking. Slowly I dragged myself back to the guesthouse. It was a long walk and my parched throat was burning raw. I couldn't speak. I headed straight for the dining room and took one of the buckets filled with ice and headed for my room. I called Morgain and in my raspy, unrecognizable voice said her name. Immediately she responded, "Raquel, that's you, I know it. I don't know what's going on but I want you to come home immediately, come straight here, do you hear me!" I needed that command. I rescheduled my flight, set the alarm and fell into a deep fitful sleep. I woke up drenched, exhausted and looked uglier than the day before. I packed and headed out. Both the plane and taxi ride were a daze.

Before I'd finished knocking, Morgain opened her door.

"What, no suntan? I thought you went to Bermuda," she said as I entered her West-side brownstone apartment.

"Would you please tell me what the hell is going on?"

"Hold me," I pleaded, "please just hold me."

We sat on the floor of her studio apartment as she cradled me in her arms, and I told her what happened, every last little detail. She drew me a hot bubble bath, sponged my back, then put me to sleep. The next day she took me to meet her therapist. I walked straight toward the woman calmly sitting behind a desk leaned over and asked in my raspy voice, "What does it mean when you unexpectedly find yourself on a cliff, seriously consider jumping off, then begin screaming so loud your blood curdles?" She didn't answer my question. Instead, she waved Morgain out and said, "Sit down. Now, let's begin at the beginning."

"At the beginning, which one? Well, it rained everyday for a week and I was stuck in my room, so I started reading my journals and . . ."

Two years after that first visit with the therapist, on my thirty-third birthday, my mother and father knelt before me with their heads on my lap weeping. I had finally told them about the horrific ten-minute experience that had distorted, reshaped, and ravaged my life and soul for the past twenty-two years. I told them how the loss of *El Piano* severed a special connection between Venus and me forever. How not graduating with my class from Walton High School, the loss of my scholarship, and our move out west had affected me. And finally, how the pain of the separation from *Alfonso* remained with me all those years, and hurt him deeply as well. I spilled my guts out for hours as they listened intently and wept continuously and asked for forgiveness. At last my secret was out.

I'd begun to let go of the pain, but it took many more years to heal from the barrage of pent-up secrets and agony I'd kept from myself, my family, my lover, my husband and friends. Slowly I peeled away the layers of melancholy that had placed me on the path toward clinical depression. A third therapist, this time a man, medication, hard work, journal writing and a few precious moments of synchronicity that brought me to writing this memoir, helped heal my deep-rooted wounds. But I learned that healing doesn't mean you forget. I still can't watch a rape scene in film or on television, or hear women and young girls being violated. Moments like that always bring back the incident, though I now have the skills to manage the memory so it doesn't take me down and keep me wallowing in that deep dark hole of unbearable pain and depression.

May used to be a month-long celebration for me beginning with the right of spring on May day, then my birthday two days later, followed by Mother's Day, and then *Mami*'s birthday. But now, Mother and Papito are gone, as is my dear friend and business partner, Sharon, who also left in May. I miss them terribly, *Mami* most of all, especially after we had worked through our differences. Even now after seventeen years I miss hearing my mother's gentle voice during our weekly phone chats, looking into her beautiful sad eyes or holding her graceful hands as we walked in the rain or strolled on the beach together. I miss discussing books and getting updated on the family happenings, or finding her that special memento from my latest trip abroad. Though as a child I resented being her personal maid, as an adult I'm glad I can manage my house and cook deliciously. Most of all, though, what remains is the abundance of encouragement and love both she and *Papito* always offered.

I see that time and age bring with them the bittersweet combination of joy coupled with sadness. Sadness at the loss of someone or something, that once brought you great joy. *Alegria y tristeza, tristeza y alegria*—joy and sadness, sadness and joy inextricably interlaced!

Yet, in spite of the melancholy interwoven with the month of May, I stand on the precipice of two wonderful milestones in my life that I intend to revel in fully. Through hard work, and many difficult lessons learned, and a few more leaps of faith taken, I'm becoming an authentic woman, who can see the loss of loved ones as an integral part of life. Losses that would not be painful, had they not first been born of love, and experienced in joy. I now focus on how far I've come, what I want to do with the next phase of my life, where I want to go, how I want to live, with love in my heart and soul fully aware of each day's blessings large and small. And, after all this time, I've come full circle, and of course, have a new book in mind and another project as well, to record my first vocal CD titled: "Boleros and Blues!"

As Simone de Beauvoir said, "One is not born a woman, one becomes one." I love the woman I'm becoming!

The End/El Fin

Gratitude and Thanks

I couldn't have come this far nor written this memoir without the help and support of many loving and trusted friends, colleagues, family, and most especially without Mother's postscript continuously resonating inside my head. Believe me, whenever I experienced writer's block and procrastinated, I'd reread that letter and got back to work.

I wish to dedicate this memoir to the three most important women in my life: my grandmother *Doña Adela*, her daughter my mother *Enedina*, and my great aunt, *Titi María*, who gave me the brilliant emerald heirloom in the silk purse. I thank my dearly departed *"chica*, friend, partner, soul mate Sharon," who, like my mother, egged me on to follow my heart and write, write, write. It was she who gave me my first book on writing by Natalie Goldberg, *Writing Down the Bones*, and then she probed, questioned, prodded, cajoled and pestered me until I finally got started. I thank my sister Venus, "the wicked witch of the West," for thinking her sister, the wicked *bruja* of the East, is a storyteller, has a good memory and a sense of humor. Though she and I have lived apart from each other since our childhood and haven't always been close, we shared wonderful moments as children with *El Piano* and our collie

Sabu. I know in my heart that in spite of it all, we love each other deeply. My thanks to her daughters, Elizabeth and Monique, who think their *"Titi"* is pretty cool. Thanks also to my first niece Angela, who sent me a beautiful pendant with the inscription, "It is the responsibility of the soul to follow its heart's desire," by Rebecca West; "I hope you follow yours" that helped me listen to my heart.

I wish to thank many women friends, beginning with Francesca-Morgain, the person who knows me the best and the longest. Then there is Inez, Eva, Kreta, *La Comay Eileen,* and Karen, my Santa Fe hiking buddy, who invited me to join her writers' group. Thanks to Myrna and Joe for helping me cleanse my soul, heal my heart and helped pay for the copy-editing of this memoir. My deepest gratitude also goes to Von and Don Quayle for including me among their family of five, and their granddaughter Summer for reading my first story. Thanks go to my nineteen National Hispana Leadership Institute sisters (NHLI) Class of 2000, and our fearless and always graceful leader, Marisa Rivera-Albert, with special thanks to classmate Antonia. Thanks to the six women of The Consulting Group—for monthly meetings that were always instructive and supportive. A special *gracias* to my Noble Roar council, they know who they are.

There were men friends who were supportive as well—most especially, Alfonso with whom I've remained close. We are fortunate to have come full circle now as friends, the kind of friends that we call family. My thanks to Dasal, Tomas, Paul my massage therapist, and Julio César, for constantly reminding me, "You can do it!"

I was fortunate and blessed to have the critical guidance of two fine editors whom I respect and offer my heartfelt gratitude and thanks: Susan Koughell and especially Jesus Treviño, a comrade throughout my media career, who generously gave his time, editorial expertise and loving support. Thanks also to Margot for the final polish.

And finally, *Gracias* to God for letting me fight with Her and not holding a grudge.